The Complete Fish Cookbook

The
COMPLETE
FISH
COOKBOOK

A CELEBRATION of SEAFOOD with RECIPES

for EVERYDAY MEALS, SPECIAL OCCASIONS, and MORE

Dani Colombatto

R

ROCKRIDGE
PRESS

For general information on our other products and services or to obtain technical support, please contact our Customer Care Department within the United States at (866) 744-2665, or outside the United States at (510) 253-0500.

Rockridge Press publishes its books in a variety of electronic and print formats. Some content that appears in print may not be available in electronic books, and vice versa.

Interior and Cover Designer: Jane Archer
Art Producer: Hannah Dickerson
Editor: Kelly Koester
Production Editor: Ruth Sakata Corley
Production Manager: Martin Worthington

Illustrations © 2021 Meel Tamphanon. Photography © Marija Vidal, pp. II, 44, 52, 141; © Darren Muir, pp. III, V, VI, X, 28, 32, 54, 63, 67, 84, 94, 99, 100, 118, 124, 127, 131, 145, 162, 166, 211, 227, 228; © Hélène Dujardin, pp. 36, 121, 194, 214; © Emulsion Studio, p. 160; © Iain Bagwell, p. 177; © Thomas Story, p. 223. Author photo courtesy of Cherece Casale Photography.

Hardcover ISBN: 978-1-63878-610-8
Paperback ISBN: 978-1-64876-499-8
eBook ISBN: 978-1-63807-570-7
R0

To the eager and earnest home cook
and the many contributors to this book.

CONTENTS

Introduction

F ew culinary categories run as deep (quite literally) as fish and seafood. From bright, gleaming red snapper to pearlescent mollusks, from tiny anchovies to tuna—to say there is a lot to navigate when it comes to seafood is an understatement. The various ways to prepare fish and the vibrant flavors of diverse regional recipes make seafood an unequivocally exciting area to explore in the home kitchen.

It seems like preparing fish has been labeled as "intimidating," and I think it's time for a rebranding. This undeserved label may be due to common misconceptions and some genuinely bad experiences. Many feel that good-quality fish is difficult to come by, perhaps due to location or budget. Some may be uncertain about the best practices concerning fishing and sustainability and unsure about what to ask when perusing the local seafood counter. Others may feel overwhelmed by the varying techniques for preparing seafood and believe that fish is too hard to handle. What if a recipe goes south, and the seafood splurge is all for naught?

All valid feelings, reader. I'm not here to minimize the depths of the, ahem, uncharted waters of cooking fish.

Although seafood territory is vast, having just a few easy, essential techniques under your belt opens up a world of opportunity. Fish is such a delicious, healthy, versatile protein. If you're not entirely confident with it yet, fear not!

I'm Dani Colombatto, a recipe developer who, you guessed it, happens to have a deep love for vibrant seafood recipes. I grew up on the coast of Southern California between Orange County and San Diego, which is, for lack of my own personal pun restraint, packed to the gills with accessible, delicious seafood. From the Mediterranean-inspired dishes I regularly ate at home, to the richly Mexican-influenced seafood I enjoyed while exploring the coast, to the late-night fodder of fried clams and fish and chips at beachside shacks, I experienced a world of flavor that forever colored the way I want to eat. With time and exploration of other cultural cuisines, seafood only got more exciting.

As you peruse these pages, you will find 115 recipes featuring a variety of cuisines, fish you can commonly find, and a bright multitude of flavors. From classic Fish and Chips (page 149) to Seafood Paella (page 167), you will discover recipes for a range of occasions and levels of home cooking experience.

My goal in this book is to shift preparing seafood from intimidating to exciting, so that it eventually works its way into your everyday recipe repertoire. Whether you're incorporating fish into your diet for health reasons or exploring new flavors and techniques, I'm confident there is a dish (and a fish) in this book for you. With that, it's time to sharpen those boning knives, stock up on the citrus, head straight for the fish counter, and cook something delicious.

1

LET'S DIVE IN

In this chapter, we get into the categories of fish—of which there are many—and talk about nuances in flavor profiles, textures, and cooking methods. We cover what to look for when seafood shopping and best practices for shopping sustainably. Additionally, we learn how to judge doneness and how to safely store, freeze, and reheat fish.

An Ode to Fish

Let's talk about health benefits first. Seafood is full of fat-based nutrients, primarily fat-soluble vitamin D. Though our bodies make most of the fats they require, omega-3 fatty acids are an exception and are essential for optimal brain and body function. They support cardiovascular health and mood health, and they lower inflammation. Because they improve skin-barrier function and moisture absorption, omega-3s even benefit hair and skin cells. These examples only scratch the surface of the benefits omega-3s offer.

RECIPES TO TRY NOW

For a family dinner: Cod in Tomato Sauce (page 130) is a decidedly light one-pan wonder. Serve it with lots of crusty bread for all that delicious sauce.

For a standout date night in: Try Grilled Lobster with Citrusy Garlic Butter (page 212), which will wow your plus-one.

If you want to grill: Rainbow Trout with Almond Butter Sauce (page 203) gives this classic a flame-kissed update that no dinner guest can resist.

For a go-to healthy recipe: Anchovy, Kale, and Salmon Caesar Salad with Lemony Bread Crumbs (page 58) is a delicious 30-minute meal that is light yet satiating.

For a cozy, comforting meal: Lobster Mac and Cheese (page 180) feels like a warm hug paired with a glass of champagne.

Understanding Fish

Within the label "seafood" lie many categories, illustrating the nuances of different types of fish. These categories are vast, so let's talk about some of the most consumed fish and seafood.

White and Flaky

Types: cod, catfish, pollock, flounder, sole, tilapia, black sea bass, haddock, hake

About: This category features mildly flavored whitefish. Delicate and flaky in texture, these fish cook quickly. Longer fillets like sole, tilapia, flounder, pollock, and catfish are classified as "thin and flaky." Cod, hake, and black sea bass are "thick and flaky." Haddock is flaky but of medium thickness.

Cooking methods: Thinner fillets are great fried, sautéed, or steamed. Thicker whitefish are a bit more forgiving texture-wise and can be baked, pan-roasted, seared, steamed, or poached.

White and Firm

Types: halibut, mahi-mahi, red snapper, swordfish, monkfish

About: These fish are meaty and hearty. Both halibut and snapper are mild in flavor, while monkfish, mahi-mahi, and swordfish are sweeter and range in texture from medium-firm to very firm. Monkfish has a delicate, sweet, lobster-like flavor, earning the moniker "poor man's lobster."

Cooking methods: Roasting is not ideal. Snapper is commonly cooked whole (see Whole Fried Snapper, page 171). Mahi-mahi, red snapper, halibut, and swordfish can all be grilled, poached, steamed, braised, or pan-seared. Monkfish is best pan-seared or braised.

Red and Fatty

Types: salmon, char

About: Salmon begin their journey in fresh water, then make their way to the ocean, returning later in life to their freshwater origins to spawn. High in omega-3s, salmon's fat content is dispersed throughout their bodies to aid their long swim. The muscle tone required to make this journey results in their firmer texture. Farmed salmon's fat content is substantially higher. Arctic char, a member of both the trout and salmon families, resembles salmon in appearance and is similar in taste to trout. Char is moderately firm and finely textured.

Cooking methods: Both can be grilled, roasted, poached, or pan-seared.

Red and Lean

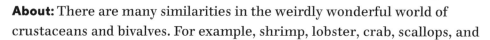

Types: tuna, trout

About: Tuna has a meaty, mild flavor, like swordfish. Tuna are leaner because they swim at a high speed, resulting in richly colored, meaty flesh with a very firm texture. Trout is flaky, medium-firm, and rich and nutty in flavor. No wonder trout almondine is a classic!

Cooking methods: Try tuna and trout grilled or pan-seared. Trout is also great roasted or steamed.

Shellfish

Types: shrimp, crab, mussels, clams, oysters, scallops, lobster

About: There are many similarities in the weirdly wonderful world of crustaceans and bivalves. For example, shrimp, lobster, crab, scallops, and oysters all possess a sweetness in flavor. While shrimp, scallops, lobster, and mussels are all tender, lobster is slightly firmer in parts and meatier, similar to scallops. Clams have a briny, "of-the-sea" flavor and are chewier in texture.

Cooking methods: Shrimp and lobster can be boiled and grilled; however, shrimp can also be poached. Enjoy mussels and clams grilled, steamed, or braised. Mussels are larger and can hold up to roasting. Oysters are usually eaten raw or grilled. Scallops can be grilled, baked, broiled, or pan-seared.

Cephalopods

Types: octopus, squid

About: These leggy relatives possess slightly chewy textures. To prepare squid, the body is typically separated from the tentacles, then the tentacles are cut in half and the body is cut crosswise into rings. Octopus is commonly found frozen. Always rinse the tentacles to remove any grit.

Cooking methods: The tougher nature of octopus means it braises well. When properly tenderized, it is also delicious grilled. Try frying squid in Fritto Misto (page 38) or marinating and grilling it.

Canned and Cured

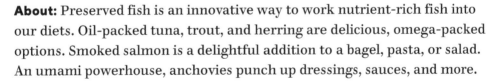

Types: tuna, sardines, mackerel, anchovies, smoked salmon

About: Preserved fish is an innovative way to work nutrient-rich fish into our diets. Oil-packed tuna, trout, and herring are delicious, omega-packed options. Smoked salmon is a delightful addition to a bagel, pasta, or salad. An umami powerhouse, anchovies punch up dressings, sauces, and more.

COOKING CHART

TYPE	HOW TO BUY	FLAVOR / TEXTURE NOTES	COOKING METHODS
ARCTIC CHAR	◆ Fresh, frozen, and previously frozen whole fish or skin-on fillets	◆ Delicate ◆ Mild, rich, trout-like	◆ Grilling ◆ Pan-searing ◆ Poaching ◆ Roasting
BLACK/ STRIPED SEA BASS	◆ Fresh whole and portioned skinless and skin-on fillets	◆ Mild, sweet ◆ Substantial flakes	◆ Baking ◆ Grilling ◆ Pan-searing ◆ Poaching ◆ Roasting ◆ Steaming
CATFISH	◆ Frozen, previously frozen, and fresh fillets	◆ Flaky, thin ◆ Mild	◆ Frying ◆ Sautéing ◆ Steaming
CLAMS	◆ Sold by bundle (in netting) or by the clam/weight ◆ Fresh or canned	◆ Chewy yet tender texture ◆ Briny, "of-the-sea" flavor with a slight sweetness	◆ Braising ◆ Grilling ◆ Steaming
COD	◆ Frozen, previously frozen, and fresh whole and portioned skinless fillets	◆ Delicate, large flakes ◆ Mild, delicate flavor	◆ Baking ◆ Pan-roasting ◆ Pan-searing ◆ Poaching ◆ Steaming

HOW TO ENJOY	BASIC PREPARATION	SUBSTITUTE WITH
Very versatile. A great swap for salmon. Works with robust flavor profiles, spices, and citrus.	Roast arctic char with Citrusy Compound Butter (page 225) at 425°F for 15 to 20 minutes, until the fish is slightly opaque.	◆ Salmon
Its clean, sweet flavor pairs well with earthy mushrooms, fennel, and citrus.	To roast, bake at 450°F for 15 minutes, or until the thickest part of the fish flakes easily. Try Pistachio-Crusted Sea Bass (page 151).	◆ Cod ◆ Haddock ◆ Hake ◆ Pollock
Excellent for frying. Try Cornmeal-Crusted Catfish Sandwiches (page 71).	Heat about 1½ inches of oil to 350°F, and fry dredged catfish fillets until golden brown and crispy, 4 to 5 minutes. Drain on a plate lined with paper towels.	◆ Flounder ◆ Sole ◆ Tilapia
Try steaming with lemon, white wine, garlic, herbs, and spices. Versatile enough to stand up to most flavor profiles and great paired with a carb of any kind.	Scrub clams. Soak clams in water with a pinch of cornmeal for 30 minutes. The clams will spit out their sand and grit. Remove each clam individually, then soak for 15 minutes more in cold water. (See White Clam Pizza on page 81 for detailed instructions.)	N/A
Cod pairs well with the sweet tomatoes in Cod in Tomato Sauce (page 130) and the citrus in Cod and Potatoes in Avgolemono (page 148).	Preheat the oven to 400°F. Pat the cod dry and place it on a baking sheet. Drizzle with olive oil or top with room-temperature Citrusy Compound Butter (page 225). Season with salt and pepper. Bake for 15 to 20 minutes.	◆ Haddock ◆ Hake ◆ Halibut ◆ Pollock ◆ Striped sea bass

TYPE	HOW TO BUY	FLAVOR / TEXTURE NOTES	COOKING METHODS
HADDOCK	◆ Frozen, previously frozen, and fresh whole and portioned skin-on fillets	◆ Delicate, mild ◆ Flaky	◆ Baking ◆ Pan-roasting ◆ Pan-searing ◆ Poaching ◆ Steaming
HALIBUT	◆ Frozen, previously frozen, and fresh whole and portioned skinless and skin-on fillets ◆ Whole belly steaks ◆ Whole steaks	◆ Rich, mild ◆ Meaty, hearty	◆ Braising ◆ Grilling ◆ Pan-searing ◆ Poaching ◆ Steaming
LOBSTER	◆ Fresh and frozen whole lobsters and lobster tails ◆ Shelled meat	◆ Tender with light chewiness in spots ◆ Meaty ◆ Medium firmness	◆ Boiling ◆ Grilling
MACKEREL	◆ Fresh whole fish ◆ Skin-on steaks ◆ Skin-on fillets ◆ Tinned, smoked, preserved	◆ Rich, full ◆ Oily, dark flesh ◆ Medium flakiness ◆ Medium firmness	◆ Broiling ◆ Grilling ◆ Roasting
MAHI-MAHI	◆ Fresh skinless steaks and fillets	◆ Sweet, robust ◆ Similar to swordfish ◆ Medium firmness ◆ Flaky, meaty	◆ Braising ◆ Grilling ◆ Pan-searing ◆ Poaching ◆ Steaming

HOW TO ENJOY	BASIC PREPARATION	SUBSTITUTE WITH
Great broiled and crusted in anything crispy, such as panko bread crumbs. It is a mild and delicate fish best served with ingredients that don't overpower it.	Season and oil the haddock. Bake at 350°F for 15 minutes.	◆ Cod ◆ Hake ◆ Pollock ◆ Striped sea bass
Halibut pairs well with fresh flavors like lemon, fennel, corn, and dill. Try Broiled Halibut with Cilantro-Corn Salad (page 139).	Drizzle the halibut with oil and season with salt and pepper. Place it on lightly oiled grill grates and grill 5 to 7 minutes. Flip, close the lid, and continue grilling until the halibut's internal temperature registers 145°F.	◆ Mahi-mahi ◆ Red snapper ◆ Striped bass ◆ Swordfish
Grilled Lobster with Citrusy Garlic Butter (page 212) is a deceptively simple take on lobster that is sure to wow any dinner guest.	Preheat a grill to medium heat. Cut the tops of the lobster shells from the meaty parts of the tails. Cut lengthwise down the center, a little less than halfway through. Insert a skewer lengthwise through the meat. Season the lobster and brush with oil. Grill, meat-side down, until charred, 5 to 6 minutes. Flip and brush with butter. Grill 4 to 5 minutes more.	N/A
Oily, robust mackerel stands up to bold flavors like ginger and peppers. Try Mackerel Piperade (page 165).	Preheat the oven to 400°F. Oil and season the fish and roast it, skin-side up, for 8 to 10 minutes, until the skin is crispy and the fillets are cooked through.	◆ Bluefish
Pair with bold and umami-rich flavors. Grilled mahi-mahi is particularly delicious, as the flame-grilled flavors are wonderful with sweet, robust mahi-mahi.	Preheat a grill to medium heat. Season the fillets and brush them with oil. Grill the mahi-mahi over direct heat with the lid closed, 4 to 5 minutes per side, until the internal temperature reaches 140°F. Cover with foil and serve at 145°F.	◆ Halibut ◆ Red snapper ◆ Striped bass ◆ Swordfish

TYPE	HOW TO BUY	FLAVOR / TEXTURE NOTES	COOKING METHODS
MONKFISH	◆ Fresh boneless, skinless loin-shaped pieces cut from the tail	◆ Similar to lobster ◆ Rich, sweet ◆ Hearty, firm	◆ Braising ◆ Pan-searing
MUSSELS	◆ Sold fresh in netting or by the mussel/weight ◆ Canned	◆ Less briny than clams ◆ Slightly sweet	◆ Braising ◆ Grilling ◆ Roasting ◆ Steaming
OCTOPUS	◆ Frozen, previously frozen, and fresh whole octopus	◆ Mild, "of-the-sea" flavor ◆ Firm ◆ Pleasantly chewy	◆ Braising ◆ Grilling, after braising or pressure-cooking to tenderize
RED SNAPPER	◆ Frozen, previously frozen, and fresh whole and portioned skin-on fillets	◆ Rich, mild ◆ Medium firmness ◆ Medium flakes	◆ Braising ◆ Grilling ◆ Pan-searing ◆ Poaching ◆ Roasting ◆ Steaming

HOW TO ENJOY	BASIC PREPARATION	SUBSTITUTE WITH
Monkfish pairs well with ingredients that typically pair well with lobster. Sear with garlicky butter for a deliciously simple dish.	Monkfish have a membrane that must be removed. Slide a boning knife (a paring or slicing knife will work, too) underneath with the blade angled upward. Using a back-and-forth motion, cut the membrane away from the fillet.	N/A
Steamed mussels with wine, garlic, herbs, and crusty bread are a classic for a reason. Check out Moules Frites (page 182).	Remove the "beard" that protrudes from the mussels before cooking. With a sharp paring knife and your thumb, firmly extract the beard from the shell, pulling toward the hinge.	N/A
Delicious when braised. Octopus Stew (page 88) is the perfect cozy recipe.	Use a sharp knife to separate the mantle and body from the head. Discard the head. Simmer the octopus in water. Use a paring knife to cut the mantle into quarters. Remove the skin and interior fibers. Remove the skin from the tentacles by pulling from the base to the tip without removing the suction cups. Cut around the body, separating the tentacles into 3 sections. Discard the center core and separate the tentacles.	N/A
Great served whole or filleted. It stands up well during grilling and fares equally well simmered to perfection in a braise.	Grill seasoned fillets over medium-high (400°F to 450°F) direct heat, 2 to 3 minutes per side, until the fish is firm to the touch and the internal temperature registers 135°F.	◆ Halibut ◆ Mahi-mahi ◆ Striped bass ◆ Swordfish

TYPE	HOW TO BUY	FLAVOR / TEXTURE NOTES	COOKING METHODS
SALMON	◆ Frozen, previously frozen, and fresh whole and portioned skin-on fillets	◆ Rich ◆ Meaty ◆ Moderate firmness ◆ Large flakes	◆ Grilling ◆ Pan-searing ◆ Poaching ◆ Roasting
SHRIMP	◆ Frozen, previously frozen, and fresh ◆ Sold by shrimp/weight	◆ Sweet ◆ Tender, juicy ◆ Moderate firmness	◆ Grilling ◆ Pan-searing ◆ Poaching
SOLE	◆ Previously frozen and fresh fillets	◆ Sweet, mild ◆ Delicate, flaky	◆ Frying ◆ Sautéing ◆ Steaming
SQUID	◆ Fresh whole bodies separated into bodies and tentacles ◆ Frozen	◆ Sweet, mild flavor ◆ Tender yet slightly chewy	◆ Braising ◆ Frying ◆ Grilling, after marinating
SWORDFISH	◆ Frozen, previously frozen, and fresh steaks	◆ Robust, meaty flavor ◆ Very firm texture	◆ Braising ◆ Grilling ◆ Pan-searing ◆ Poaching ◆ Steaming

HOW TO ENJOY	BASIC PREPARATION	SUBSTITUTE WITH
Grilling is a popular preparation method. Pan-searing creates perfectly crispy skin.	Pat the fillets dry and season them. Drizzle 2 tablespoons of oil in a cast-iron skillet. Place the salmon skin-side down in the skillet while it is still heating. Cook the salmon, occasionally recirculating the fat under the fillets to crisp the skin. Cook until opaque up the sides of the fillets, 6 to 10 minutes. Flip the fillets and turn off the heat. Transfer the fish to a plate once the sizzling stops.	◆ Arctic char
Shrimp on the grill followed up with plentiful brushes of butter or pan-seared in a flavorful sauce are delightful.	Heat 2 tablespoons of oil on high in a large skillet. Season the shrimp, place them flat-side down, and cook, undisturbed, for 1 minute. Flip and cook for 1 minute more.	N/A
Sole is great crispy and paired with lemon. Try Parmigiano-Crusted Sole with Pesto Orzo (page 186) or Sole Meunière (page 140).	Preheat the oven to 425°F. Line a baking sheet with parchment paper and brush with olive oil. After dredging the sole, place the fillets on the baking sheet and drizzle each with ½ tablespoon of oil. Bake for 20 minutes, or until golden brown. Try this method for flounder fillets, too.	◆ Catfish ◆ Flounder ◆ Tilapia
Delicious marinated and grilled or fried and paired with lots of lemon. Try Fritto Misto (page 38).	In a large Dutch oven over medium heat, heat 3 inches of oil to 350°F. Fry the squid in batches until golden brown, about 2 to 3 minutes. Drain on a plate lined with paper towels.	N/A
Swordfish's meatiness pairs well with bold flavors. Delicious when grilled or seared.	Season the swordfish and brush with olive oil. Grill until it lifts off the grates without sticking and there are distinct grill marks, 5 to 6 minutes per side. Top the steaks with 1 tablespoon of Citrusy Compound Butter (page 225), cover with foil, and let rest for 5 minutes before serving.	◆ Halibut ◆ Mahi-mahi ◆ Red snapper ◆ Striped bass

TYPE	HOW TO BUY	FLAVOR / TEXTURE NOTES	COOKING METHODS
TILAPIA	◆ Frozen, previously frozen, and fresh fillets	◆ Mild flavor ◆ Very thin fillets ◆ Firm, flaky texture	◆ Frying ◆ Sautéing ◆ Steaming
TROUT	◆ Previously frozen and fresh whole fish and portioned fillets	◆ Rich, nutty flavor ◆ Medium firmness ◆ Flaky	◆ Grilling ◆ Pan-searing ◆ Roasting ◆ Steaming
TUNA	◆ Frozen, previously frozen, and fresh steaks ◆ Canned	◆ Firm, meaty ◆ Mild flavor ◆ Deeply colored	◆ Grilling ◆ Pan-searing

Shopping for Fish

Whether you're shopping for fresh or frozen, for fillets or whole fish, there are many factors to consider to ensure you select a fish you will enjoy. Buying fish does not have to break the bank, and there are accessible best choices—you just need to know what to look for.

HOW TO ENJOY	BASIC PREPARATION	SUBSTITUTE WITH
The thinness of tilapia fillets makes them ideal for frying. Swap in tilapia anywhere you would use sole, catfish, or flounder.	Heat a large skillet over high heat until smoking. Add 2 tablespoons of canola oil, immediately followed by the seasoned tilapia fillets, gently shaking the skillet occasionally to redistribute the fat. Cook until the fish is golden brown, 3 minutes. Flip and cook for 1 minute more.	◆ Catfish ◆ Flounder ◆ Sole
Rainbow Trout with Almond Butter Sauce (page 203) highlights the inherent nuttiness of the trout.	Heat 1 to 2 tablespoons of canola oil in a skillet over medium-high heat. When the oil is hot, place the seasoned trout in the skillet, skin-side down. Sear for 6 minutes. Carefully flip the fillets and cook for 1 to 2 minutes more.	◆ Arctic char
Best seared at high heat, leaving the internal temperature rare. Sushi-grade tuna is also delicious raw.	Preheat a grill to medium-high heat (400°F to 450°F). Oil and season the steaks, then grill over direct heat, 2 minutes per side, until golden brown. The inside should remain rare.	N/A

Fresh

How to spot a fresh fish steak or fillet:

- The fish is homogenous in color.

- It has a bright, shiny surface.

- If you press your index finger into the flesh, it springs back and does not leave an indentation.

- The flesh is firm and pliable.

Fish should never smell fishy but should register as lightly sweet and "of the ocean." Fillets and steaks should always be sold on ice but not buried in it. Burying fillets in ice impacts their texture, making them mealy and unpleasant.

Whole Fish

Whole fish should be entirely buried in ice with no visible damage to the skin. They should be bright and iridescent from a natural substance present in fresh fish that protects their skin. Check for clear eyes. If the eyes are sunken or cloudy, do not purchase the fish. The flesh should be firm, and the gills should be moist and red.

Shellfish

All the shells of clams, oysters, and mussels should be closed. Tap any that are slightly open. They should shut. If they do not, they are dead and must be discarded. They should smell "of the ocean," and the shells should be free of mud, dirt, and debris. Shellfish should be buried in ice in the display case, as their shells protect the flesh from damage.

Shell-on shrimp tend to be handled less. They should smell "of the ocean," slightly sweet. The flesh should appear firm and feel clean.

Scallops range from pearlescent white to pale pink and should smell somewhat briny, not sharp, of iodine, or of nothing at all.

Frozen

Some frozen options might be of better quality than those at the fresh seafood counter. Why? Many varieties are frozen on the boat using advanced methods to preserve them at the time of catch. When we buy fish preserved at the time of catch, we benefit from more of their vitamins and minerals. Here are a few points to keep in mind when selecting frozen fish:

* Check the packaging for any tears, holes, or punctures. These allow air and moisture in, which causes ice to form and break down the fish's flesh.

- There should be no liquid inside the packaging.

- The flesh should be firm.

- To defrost the fish, remove them from all packaging and place them in the refrigerator overnight. If the fish is sealed, you can thaw it by placing it in a bowl of ice water in the refrigerator, changing the water every 30 minutes.

- Never thaw fish in the microwave.

Sushi-Grade

There is much debate about what "sushi-grade" means. Although there are currently no official guidelines for what constitutes sushi- or sashimi-grade fish, this label means the fish is "safe" to eat raw. This applies to whole marine fish. If this term is assigned to freshwater varieties, they were previously frozen to kill any parasites.

Canned and Cured

There are endless varieties of delicious canned and cured fish. Look for BPA-free cans (most of them are). If you're buying oil-packed fish, look for olive oil and check the ingredients. Some say olive oil but include other oils, such as canola or soybean oil. Look for labels that denote wild-caught or sustainably harvested fish. For great tuna options, check out the brands Wild Planet and Cole's Seafood, both of which are certified by the Aquaculture Stewardship Council (ASC).

Seasonality

Just like some produce may be unavailable at your local farmers' market because it's out of season, certain types of wild fish are not always available. Like most foods, fish, too, have a season.

From an ecological standpoint, if fisheries operated according to seasonality, they would distribute their fishing impact more evenly versus operating off primarily what is in demand. Shopping according to seasonality can help alleviate the demand for out-of-season, overfished seafood.

Mercury and Other Health Concerns

Mercury is absorbed in fish via bioaccumulation. When chemicals and toxins settle in the underwater sediment, macroinvertebrates ingest them while eating. Larger creatures, in turn, eat those macroinvertebrates, thereby consuming that toxin, and the cycle continues with each slightly larger fish that gets ingested. Longer-living predators contain more of these toxins. Why? They eat a lot of smaller fish.

To help guide mindful consumption, Monterey Bay Aquarium's Seafood Watch breaks down seafood according to mercury level to help us determine what we should be consuming less frequently.

WILD VS. FARMED

This is a layered topic and one all seafood lovers should educate themselves on. Many questions arise when deciding between wild-caught and farmed fish. Where is the fish coming from? How was it caught or raised? If it was farmed, were additives used? Wild fish are not as prone to harmful contaminants, and they are never treated with antibiotics.

While wild salmon is available from spring to early fall, farmed salmon is produced all year long. These farms are located mostly in the Atlantic, while wild salmon comes primarily from the Pacific Ocean. Farmed salmon does not benefit from a crustacean-rich diet and in some cases is fed a synthetic carotenoid pigment for color. Farmed salmon is richer and more buttery due to its collagen and higher fat content, which is the result of being less active than wild salmon, which is leaner and firmer due to its active life.

GONE (SUSTAINABLY) FISHING

The issue of overfishing and invasive fishing methods endangering wildlife and ecosystems must be acknowledged. The big business of fishing has muddied the waters of ethics when it comes to purchasing seafood. Thankfully, many markets care about where their seafood comes from—down to the boat—and transparently share this information with customers. Aquaculture (farmed fish) has made it possible for us to control fishing's environmental impact. Resources like Monterey Bay Aquarium's Seafood Watch provide excellent, up-to-date information on sustainability and aquaculture, as well as other news and a host of resources on best practices for purchasing sustainable fish, including details on how they are caught.

5 TIPS FOR BEST SUSTAINABILITY PRACTICES

1. **Investigate your source.** Ask, "Is this sustainable?" Responsible companies are well-informed on where their seafood is coming from, and it should not be difficult for you to find out more information.

2. **Buy in season when possible.** Buying in season allows fisheries to distribute the environmental impact of fishing more equally.

3. **Buy locally when possible.** Shopping locally increases traceability and transparency. You'll know when and where the fish was caught. You'll also benefit from peak taste and freshness and a shorter supply chain, and you'll support your local economy.

4. **Go small.** Some species of fish, such as sardines, mackerel, anchovies, and herring, exist in larger quantities and are underutilized. Their populations replenish more rapidly than those of larger fish, so they are a great option to help relieve demand.

5. **Look for a label.** Some certification labels denote responsible seafood practices and environmentally friendly choices: ASC (Aquaculture Stewardship Council), MSC (Marine Stewardship Council), and BAP (Best Aquaculture Practices).

FISH TO CONSIDER

What makes a particular fish a great choice, a good choice, or one to avoid depends heavily on the location where it's caught and the fishing method used. In this chart, you will see some of the same species in more than one column. Please refer to Monterey Bay Aquarium's Seafood Watch Consumer Guide for detailed location and fishing method information.

GREAT	GOOD	RETHINK
US Farmed Fish:	**US Farmed Fish:**	**US Farmed Fish:**
Catfish, tilapia, barramundi, rainbow trout, coho salmon, butter sole, hybrid red tilapia	Atlantic cod, sockeye salmon, black sea bass, Dover sole	Endangered species: Bluefin tuna, shark, Chilean sea bass, orange roughy, black sea bass
US Wild-Caught:	**US Wild-Caught:**	**US Wild-Caught:**
Alaskan salmon, arctic char, sardines, halibut, white seabass, arrowtooth flounder, haddock, pollock, Chinook salmon, coho salmon, sockeye salmon, blue striped snapper, Dover sole, English sole, lake trout, albacore tuna, walleye	Black grouper, Pacific halibut, Atlantic herring, black marlin, opah, blue striped snapper, gray snapper, red snapper, swordfish, lake trout, albacore tuna	Black grouper, Atlantic halibut, Atlantic mackerel, black marlin, opah, red snapper, lake trout, albacore tuna, walleye
US Wild Shellfish:	**US Wild Shellfish:**	**US Wild Shellfish:**
Atlantic lobster; Maine lobster; blue mussels; Eastern oysters; American, Atlantic, Digby and Hotate scallops; ocean shrimp	Blue mussels, Eastern oysters, bay scallops, Pacific calico scallops, pink shrimp, royal red shrimp, Atlantic seabob shrimp, brown rock shrimp	Atlantic seabob shrimp, brown rock shrimp, Pacific rock shrimp, pink shrimp, white shrimp
US Farmed Shellfish:	**US Farmed Shellfish:**	
Oysters, clams, mussels, blue shrimp	Blue shrimp, giant freshwater prawns, giant tiger prawns	

GREAT: These are caught or farmed responsibly.
GOOD: There are some concerns with how these are caught, farmed, or managed.
RETHINK: These are overfished or caught/farmed in ways that are harmful to the environment.

Prepping Fish

Cleaning and filleting are undoubtedly intimidating aspects of cooking seafood. However, they are much more straightforward and, frankly, less scary than one might think.

How to Clean and Fillet a Whole Fish

1. Have a fishmonger scale and gut the whole fish and remove the fins.

2. To fillet, lay the fish on a work surface and pat dry. With a boning knife, score a cut at the tail of the fish. Slice around the head, cutting through until the knife hits bones.

3. With the flat of the knife along the fish's backbone, slice lengthwise along the backbone, from head to tail. With the knife's tip, gradually slice the fillet away, making gentle, sweeping cuts. Work from the backbone to the belly. At the belly, cut the fillet away from the fish.

4. Flip the fish over and repeat the previous steps to remove the second fillet. Trim the fillets of excess fat.

How to Remove Pin Bones

When you purchase a fillet, the larger ribs and backbone will already be removed, but the thin pin bones will remain and can be removed separately.

Place the fillet on top of a mixing bowl turned upside down; this will help the pin bones protrude from the surface. Use your fingers to gently feel for bones. Using a pair of tweezers, with a firm grasp, slowly and steadily extract each pin bone from the flesh. Pay attention to the angle the pin bone is naturally pointing, and pull in that general direction to prevent tearing the flesh.

How to Skin

Some species of fish—such as salmon, mackerel, bass, flounder, and snapper—are known for having skin that's delicious when crisped up. Some recipes, though, require skinless fish.

To skin a fillet, begin at the corner. Using the tip of a sharp boning knife (or a very sharp chef's knife), cut the skin away from the flesh. About halfway through, utilize your other hand to pull the skin away from the fillet, exposing more flesh and making it easier to cut away the skin.

EQUIPMENT ESSENTIALS

Making delicious fish at home requires only a few tools that will undoubtedly get utilized time and again.

A great skillet: A large, stainless-steel skillet is an essential tool for fish (and other dishes). Since it distributes heat evenly, it is excellent for searing, and it won't transfer anything strange into the food, like some nonstick skillets do. Cast-iron skillets are workhorses in the kitchen and are so versatile. An enameled cast-iron pot, like a Dutch oven, is ideal for multiple jobs, such as searing seafood before making a large stew.

A fish spatula: A long spatula with an angled edge, a fish spatula makes it easy to flip and remove fillets from the cooking pan without tearing the flesh.

A boning knife: With long, narrow blades and thin cross-sections, boning knives leave very little waste, cleanly removing meat from connective tissue and bone without damaging the muscle.

An oyster knife: Made with strong and durable blades, oyster knives withstand the pressure of shucking open an oyster shell, making the job easier and undeniably safer.

Cooking Fish

Let's talk about some of the most utilized techniques for cooking fish and seafood, as well as some tips and tricks for a successful outcome.

Roasting

High-temperature roasting is a popular hands-off, versatile method of cooking fish. Whole fish greatly benefit from the browning and flavor development that occurs when roasting. Fish skin becomes crispy with the help of a preheated baking sheet. Breaded fillets are crisped to perfection without frying. Since roasting can dry out a protein, it's best to use oily fish for this method. Flaky whitefish like halibut or cod tend to dry out if cooked without enough liquid.

Baking

This is a lower-temperature oven method, perfect for delicate, flaky fish. This gentler method cooks the protein gradually, allowing flavors to be imparted to the fish. Baking is a great method for dishes like Pistachio-Crusted Sea Bass (page 151), where we want a crispy crust and succulent fillets.

Sautéing and Searing

Excellent for preserving texture, moisture, and flavor, sautéing and searing develops flavor on the bottom of the pan and color on the fish and is an option for almost any fillet.

Broiling

High-heat broiling is an excellent option for fish when you want extra golden color on the exterior surface. This method is ideal for any fish with a high oil content, as they are less likely to dry out.

Steaming

This is a delicious method that gently cooks the fish while imparting delicious flavors, like the aromatics in Garlicky White Wine–Steamed Clams (page 142). It's also a healthy method that cooks fish uniformly. When fish is cooked uncovered, some of its moisture escapes through vapor. By trapping that vapor, we retain the fish's moisture, resulting in a rich, never-dry outcome.

Poaching

Another gentle, moisture-retaining method, this involves submerging the fish in a liquid. Classic French techniques involve cooking liquids infused with aromatics like herbs and vegetables whose flavors get imparted into the fish. Oil-poaching is another delicious option.

Braising

If you're looking to tenderize, braising is the best choice. A fantastic match for octopus or squid, this method uses gentle cooking in an enclosed environment to slowly break down the protein, and the results are impossibly tender. This slow-paced method is wonderful for fish stews and chowders, as it allows them to develop rich flavor profiles.

Frying

This quick-cooking method is a favorite for everything from cornmeal-crusted catfish to battered calamari in a Fritto Misto (page 38). A 350°F temperature using avocado oil yields the best results.

Grilling

The flame-licked flavor imparted by the grill to the fish is unmatched and is the reason many love seafood. For no-stick fillets, an oiled grill grate is your best friend. Before grilling fish, fold paper towels up and dip them in a cooking oil with

TIP

If your fish still sticks, slide a fish spatula between the skin and the fillet, gently removing the fillet from the skin and onto a plate. Chances are, no one will be the wiser.

a high smoke point. Wipe the grate, then repeat twice more. Allow the grill to preheat, then repeat once more before grilling.

Curing

Curing fish typically involves a mixture of salt, sugar, spices, and sometimes even alcohol. Fish is rubbed in the spice mixture, wrapped tightly, refrigerated (usually while placed under a heavy object), and cured for 36 to 72 hours. The longer the cure, the saltier and firmer the fish will be.

JUDGING DONENESS

Fish can be fickle when it comes to visually clocking doneness. It might appear opaque enough on the outside, but the center could still resemble something akin to sashimi. So, it helps to know several indicators of doneness.

Sight: The flesh should appear opaque. If you stick a paring knife into the center of the fillet at an angle, the flesh should flake easily.

Touch and feel: Tap the flesh with your finger to determine the separation of flakes. When you poke the flesh, the firmness should resemble the tip of your nose. Determining this will become easier with practice.

Temperature: A properly calibrated instant-read thermometer is a great way to test for doneness. Insert the thermometer into the thickest part of the flesh (if using a whole fish, away from the backbone); the ideal temperature range is between 125°F and 140°F. You'll want to remove the fish from the heat when the internal temperature reaches 135°F to avoid overcooking it.

Storing and Reheating Fish

Certain practices ensure quality reheated seafood, and spoiler—none of them involve a microwave. When it comes to reheating in the oven, thicker fillets are more forgiving, as they're less likely to dry out. Though salmon reheats well the next day, reheating makes salmon's inherent flavor more pronounced, so it makes a better cold addition to dishes like pasta salads.

In addition to the following table that outlines guidelines for how long to freeze and refrigerate fish, here are some things to keep in mind:

- Moisture is the enemy when it comes to freezing fish, as ice crystals will hurt the texture of fish fillets.

- Double wrap fish in plastic wrap followed by parchment and foil (or vacuum seal) before freezing.

- Reheating in foil at 275°F for 15 minutes will bring the fish's temperature up to the desired range without drying it out.

- Keep refrigerator temperatures at 40°F or less.

- Never refreeze thawed fish.

	REFRIGERATE	FREEZE
Fresh oily fish (whole)	2 to 3 days	1½ to 2 months
Fresh oily fish (fillets and steaks)	2 to 3 days	1 to 1½ months
Fresh lean fish (whole)	2 to 3 days	4 to 6 months
Fresh lean fish (fillets and steaks)	2 to 3 days	3 to 4 months
Frozen fish	Within 24 hours of thawing	3 to 6 months
Cooked fish	3 to 4 days	1 month

2

SMALL PLATES

The Easiest Shrimp Cocktail

SERVES 4

PREP TIME:
15 minutes

COOK TIME:
10 minutes

In this new take on a classic, shrimp get oven-roasted and then paired with a zippy cocktail sauce.

FOR THE COCKTAIL SAUCE

⅓ cup sriracha

½ cup ketchup

2 tablespoons prepared
  horseradish

Juice of ½ lemon

½ teaspoon Worcestershire
  sauce

FOR THE SHRIMP

2 pounds extra-jumbo (U16/20)
  shrimp, tail-on, peeled, and
  deveined

1½ tablespoons extra-virgin
  olive oil

2 teaspoons kosher salt

½ teaspoon freshly ground
  black pepper

TIP

For a Cajun-style shrimp cocktail, add 2 teaspoons of Cajun seasoning or Old Bay to the marinade.

TO MAKE THE COCKTAIL SAUCE

1. In a small bowl, stir together the sriracha, ketchup, horseradish, lemon juice, and Worcestershire sauce. Cover the bowl with plastic wrap and refrigerate until ready to use.

TO MAKE THE SHRIMP

2. Preheat the oven to 400°F. Line a baking sheet with aluminum foil or parchment paper.

3. In a small bowl, toss the shrimp with the olive oil, salt, and pepper. Let the shrimp marinate for 5 minutes. Spread the shrimp out in a single layer on the prepared baking sheet.

4. Roast for 10 minutes, until the shrimp turn pink and opaque white. Remove from the oven and set aside to cool.

5. Smear a spoonful of sauce onto each of four chilled plates. Evenly divide the shrimp among the plates and serve immediately.

Octopus Salad

SERVES 4

PREP TIME:
20 minutes

This recipe calls for canned octopus because fresh octopus can be hard to source depending on where you live. Canned octopus is available online and at most stores now, and it tastes excellent in this recipe. If you have access to quality fresh octopus, feel free to use that instead.

FOR THE SALAD

1 (8-ounce) can precooked octopus

½ green bell pepper, seeded and chopped

½ red bell pepper, seeded and chopped

½ red onion, diced

1 small tomato, chopped

FOR THE DRESSING

1 tablespoon extra-virgin olive oil

1 tablespoon white wine vinegar

1 garlic clove, minced

Juice of ½ lime

Kosher salt

TO MAKE THE SALAD

1. Drain and rinse the octopus, pat it dry, and cut it into bite-size pieces. In a large bowl, toss together the octopus, green and red peppers, onions, and tomatoes.

TO MAKE THE DRESSING

2. In a small bowl, whisk together the olive oil, vinegar, garlic, lime juice, and salt to taste. Drizzle the dressing over the salad and toss to coat evenly.

TIP

To use fresh octopus, place it in a pot and cover with salted water. Bring to a simmer over medium-high heat, cover, and cook for about 1 hour. Allow the octopus to cool, then clean and slice it before adding it to the salad.

TIP

Lump crabmeat goes great with avocado. Substitute ½ cup of crabmeat in place of salmon.

Smoked Salmon with Baked Eggs in Avocados

SERVES 4

PREP TIME:
10 minutes

COOK TIME:
15 minutes

Buttery avocado, runny eggs, smoked salmon, and toast— what more could you need? Garnish this delicious dish with minced chives, fresh parsley, or cilantro.

2 extra-large avocados
Kosher salt
Freshly ground black pepper
2 ounces smoked salmon
4 large eggs
Pinch red pepper flakes
  (optional)

1 tablespoon extra-virgin
  olive oil, for drizzling
Lemon wedges, for serving
4 slices sourdough bread,
  toasted

1. Preheat the oven to 400°F.

2. Cut the avocados in half and carefully remove the pits. Use a spoon to remove one or two scoops of the inside of the avocados to make larger cavities for the eggs. Reserve the scooped-out avocado for serving with the toast.

3. Place the avocados in an 8-by-8-inch baking dish. Season them with a pinch each of salt and pepper. Divide the smoked salmon slices between the avocado halves. Break the eggs carefully into the avocados over the salmon and season lightly with more salt and pepper. Sprinkle lightly with the red pepper flakes (if using).

4. Bake for 12 to 14 minutes, until the egg whites set but the yolks are still runny.

5. Drizzle the tops of the eggs with the olive oil. Serve each avocado with lemon wedges and toast.

Avocado Boats with Crabmeat and Creole Salsa

MAKES 16 BOATS

PREP TIME:
10 minutes

This fresh, bright appetizer comes together in a flash with fresh avocados, lump crabmeat, and a sprinkling of Cajun Spice Blend.

4 avocados
½ pound fresh lump crabmeat
½ cup Creole Salsa (page 216)

1 tablespoon Cajun Spice Blend (page 217) or store-bought

1. Cut each avocado in half lengthwise, remove the pit, and cut each half lengthwise again. Repeat with the remaining avocados until you have 16 avocado boats.

2. Place 1 tablespoon of crabmeat in the center of each avocado boat, then top with ½ tablespoon of Creole salsa. Arrange the boats on a serving platter and sprinkle evenly with the Cajun spice blend. Serve immediately.

TIP

You cannot make these ahead of time, but sprinkle a bit of fresh lemon juice over the avocados if you need to prep them before serving. Doing so will help prevent the avocados from oxidizing, which makes them brown and mushy.

Citrusy Red Snapper Ceviche

**SERVES
2 TO 4**

PREP TIME:
25 minutes

If you've ever enjoyed the bright beachy glory that is ceviche but have yet to make it at home, you might be surprised at how quickly it comes together. Seek out homemade tortilla chips for serving; they make all the difference.

5 tablespoons freshly
  squeezed lime juice
2 tablespoons freshly
  squeezed orange juice
1 large garlic clove, minced
Pinch kosher salt
1 pound red snapper, cut into
  ½-inch pieces
1 cup heirloom cherry
  tomatoes, thinly sliced

½ small red onion, minced
½ small serrano pepper,
  seeded and minced
1½ tablespoons extra-virgin
  olive oil
1 avocado, peeled, pitted, and
  cut into ½-inch dice
¾ cup chopped fresh cilantro
¼ cup toasted pepitas
Tortilla chips, for serving

1. In a medium bowl, whisk together the lime juice, orange juice, garlic, and salt. Add the snapper, gently tossing to combine. Let the fish sit, stirring occasionally to ensure all the fish gets in the marinade, until the fish firms up a bit, about 15 minutes.

2. Add the tomatoes, onion, serrano pepper, and olive oil and gently toss to combine. Let sit for 5 minutes.

3. Gently fold in the avocado and cilantro and sprinkle with the pepitas. Serve with tortilla chips.

TIP

For a spicy kick,
add between ¼ and
½ teaspoon of
horseradish
or sriracha.

Coconut Crab Cakes

SERVES 4

PREP TIME:
15 minutes,
plus 1 hour
to chill

COOK TIME:
10 minutes

These lightly tropical, golden crab cakes are delicious alongside a heaping spoonful of mango salsa, a swipe of garlic aioli, or a bright and spicy guacamole. To create a delectable sandwich, double the patty size and serve with crispy lettuce and ripe tomato on a crusty bun.

1 pound canned lump
  crabmeat, drained and
  picked over
¼ cup coconut flour
1 scallion, white and green
  parts, finely chopped
1 large egg, beaten

½ teaspoon minced garlic
Zest and juice of ½ lemon
Sea salt
Freshly ground black pepper
2 tablespoons extra-virgin
  olive oil

1. In a medium bowl, mix the crabmeat, coconut flour, scallion, egg, garlic, lemon zest, and lemon juice. Season with salt and pepper.

2. Divide the crab mixture into 8 portions and form them into cakes about 1 inch thick.

3. Chill the crab cakes, covered, in the refrigerator for 1 hour so they firm up.

4. Heat the olive oil in a large skillet over medium-high heat.

5. Sear the crab cakes until they are golden on both sides, turning once, about 5 minutes per side.

6. Store leftover crab cakes in a sealed container in the refrigerator for up to 2 days.

Fritto Misto

SERVES 6

PREP TIME:
10 minutes

COOK TIME:
20 minutes

This delicate and light batter allows the seafood to really shine.

¾ cup mayonnaise

Zest of 1 lemon

2 tablespoons freshly
squeezed lemon juice

2 tablespoons capers, drained

1 large garlic clove, minced

2 tablespoons extra-virgin
olive oil

½ teaspoon kosher salt, plus
more for seasoning

Freshly ground black pepper

Safflower oil, for frying

¾ cup all-purpose flour

¼ cup rice flour

1 cup cornstarch

1 teaspoon baking powder

2 cups cold wheat beer
or 1 (16-ounce) bottle cold
club soda

8 ounces squid or baby
octopus tentacles

8 ounces shrimp, tail-on,
peeled, and deveined

1 lemon, cut into wedges

1. In a small bowl, whisk together the mayonnaise, lemon zest, lemon juice, capers, and garlic. While whisking, stream in the olive oil. Season generously with salt and pepper. Cover and refrigerate until ready to eat.

2. In a large Dutch oven over medium-high heat, heat 4 inches of safflower oil to 350°F. Line a baking sheet with paper towels.

3. In a large bowl, whisk together the all-purpose flour, rice flour, cornstarch, baking powder, and ½ teaspoon of salt. While whisking, pour in the beer. The batter should have a very thin consistency.

4. Working in batches, dip the squid and shrimp in the batter and carefully add it to the hot oil. Fry, gently turning and separating, until evenly golden and crisp, 1 to 3 minutes. Using a slotted spoon, transfer to a paper towel–lined baking sheet. Season with salt and serve with the lemon wedges and the lemon-caper aioli.

Clams Casino

SERVES 4

PREP TIME:
20 minutes

COOK TIME:
25 minutes

Though this recipe originated in Rhode Island, you can find it on nearly every menu in New York City's Little Italy. A truly old-school dinner party favorite, this dish can be prepared ahead of time and popped in the oven just before the guests arrive.

12 littleneck clams, scrubbed well under cold water

¼ cup water

4 bacon slices, cut widthwise into ¼-inch strips

1 tablespoon unsalted butter

1 (4-ounce) jar diced pimentos, drained

1 small shallot, minced

2 garlic cloves, minced

Kosher salt

Freshly ground black pepper

¾ cup panko bread crumbs

1 tablespoon roughly chopped fresh oregano leaves

1 tablespoon minced fresh parsley

1 tablespoon grated Parmigiano-Reggiano cheese

1 lemon, cut into wedges

1. Put the clams in a medium saucepan and pour the water over them. Cover and turn the heat to medium-high. Steam the clams for 6 to 7 minutes, or until they've all completely opened. Remove the pan from the heat and set it aside to cool slightly.

2. Set a bowl on the counter to catch any juice that runs out of the clams as you shell them. When the clams are cool enough to handle, remove the top shell of each clam (the deeper shell is the bottom one) and run a spoon under the meat of the clam to dislodge it from the shell and turn it over. (This will make it much easier to spear with a fork and eat.) Arrange the clams in their bottom shells in a single layer in a 9-by-13-inch baking dish. Strain the clam juice and set it aside.

Continued on next page ⟶

3. In a large nonstick, oven-safe skillet over medium-high heat, cook the bacon until just browned but not yet crisp, 5 to 6 minutes. Use a slotted spoon to transfer the bacon to a paper towel–lined plate and set aside. Discard the bacon fat, but do not discard the brown buildup from the bacon clinging to the skillet.

4. Return the skillet to medium-high heat and melt the butter. Sauté the pimentos, shallot, and garlic for about 4 minutes. Season lightly with salt and pepper. Add 2 tablespoons of the reserved clam juice to deglaze the skillet. Continue cooking until the clam juice has evaporated, about 2 minutes. Turn off the heat and set the skillet aside to cool.

5. Preheat the oven to broil.

6. Return the skillet to your work surface and stir in the bread crumbs, oregano, parsley, and cheese. Divide this mixture between the clams. Top with the bacon strips.

7. Broil the dish for 3 to 5 minutes, or until the bacon is crispy and the bread crumbs are toasted and golden. Squeeze the lemon over the clams and serve immediately.

TIP

Using mussels instead of clams turns this dish into Mussels au Gratin. Mussels are much smaller than littleneck clams, so prepare twice as many and cook them for half the time.

Crispy Rice and Ahi Bites

**SERVES
4 TO 6**

Crispy cakes of sushi rice get topped with bright, spicy ahi studded with scallions and sesame seeds.

PREP TIME:
30 minutes,
plus time
to cool and
1 hour to
freeze

COOK TIME:
40 minutes

1½ cups sushi rice, thoroughly
   rinsed
3 cups water
1½ teaspoons salt
1 pound sushi-grade ahi, fresh
   or frozen and defrosted, cut
   into ½-inch dice
4 scallions, white and green
   parts, sliced
1 tablespoon mayonnaise

1½ teaspoons sriracha
1 teaspoon sesame seeds
1 teaspoon sesame oil
1 teaspoon soy sauce
1 tablespoon rice wine vinegar
½ teaspoon freshly squeezed
   lemon juice
½ cup all-purpose flour
3 tablespoons avocado oil

TIP

*Well-rinsed rice
is the key to
properly cooked
sushi rice.*

1. In a medium saucepan, combine the rice, water, and salt. Bring to a boil, then reduce the heat to low, cover, and cook for 20 minutes. Cool completely.

2. Cover a 9-by-13-inch baking dish with a layer of plastic wrap. Allow for enough overhang to wrap over the entire dish. Transfer the rice to the baking dish and firmly press into an even layer. Tightly cover with plastic wrap and freeze for 1 hour.

3. In a medium bowl, toss the tuna, scallions, mayonnaise, sriracha, sesame seeds, sesame oil, soy sauce, vinegar, and lemon juice. Cover with plastic wrap and refrigerate until ready to serve.

4. Place the flour in a shallow baking dish. Cut the rice into 1½-by-2-inch rectangles. Dust all sides of the rice with flour.

5. In a large skillet over medium-high heat, heat the avocado oil. Once the oil is hot, work in batches and fry the rice rectangles on all sides until golden brown, 1 to 2 minutes per side. Transfer the rectangles to a paper towel–lined plate to cool.

6. Top the rice cakes with the ahi mixture and serve.

Oysters Mornay

SERVES 4

PREP TIME:
25 minutes

COOK TIME:
10 minutes

Mornay sauce is a French cooking staple, and here it's spooned onto freshly shucked oysters and broiled to bubbly perfection. These classic broiled oysters make a special appetizer, especially served with a flute of bubbles on a cool night.

FOR THE MORNAY SAUCE

3 tablespoons unsalted butter
3 tablespoons all-purpose flour
1 cup whole milk
½ teaspoon Espelette pepper or sweet paprika
1 teaspoon sea salt
Pinch grated nutmeg
½ cup shredded Gruyère cheese

FOR THE OYSTERS

2 cups sel gris or rock salt
24 live oysters
¼ cup panko bread crumbs

TO MAKE THE MORNAY SAUCE

1. In a small saucepan over medium heat, melt the butter until foamy. Add the flour and whisk until the mixture is foamy, about 3 minutes. Gradually add the milk, whisking until the mixture is smooth.

2. Reduce the heat to low and cook, stirring constantly, until the sauce is thick, about 3 minutes. Stir in the Espelette pepper, salt, and nutmeg and remove the pan from the heat. Stir in the Gruyère.

TO MAKE THE OYSTERS

3. Preheat the oven to broil. Pour the sel gris on an oven-safe serving tray to create a bed.

4. Shuck the oysters, draining any seawater into the sauce as you go. Arrange the oysters on the bed of salt, discarding the top shells. Evenly spoon the sauce over each oyster and sprinkle with the bread crumbs.

5. Broil the oysters until brown and bubbly, about 5 minutes. Serve immediately.

TIP

Look for small, deep-cupped oysters with a harder shell. If buying from a fish market, ask for beach-tumbled oysters; these are grown closer to a beach, where the waves constantly tumble them, strengthening the shell and making the oyster grow with a deep cup and a more rounded shape. These oysters are also easier to open. Larger-scale oyster fishermen will use a machine that simulates the wave action to get the same results.

Oysters Rockefeller

**SERVES
4 TO 6**

PREP TIME:
10 minutes

COOK TIME:
35 minutes

This dish was created by Jules Alciatore in 1899 and named after John D. Rockefeller—the richest American at the time—some say because of the richness of the sauce, others because the spinach represents the color of money.

1 tablespoon unsalted butter
½ cup minced onion
1 celery stalk, minced
1½ teaspoons minced garlic
1 pound frozen chopped
  spinach, thawed and
  squeezed dry
1 ounce anisette liqueur,
  Herbsaint, or Pernod
1 teaspoon dry mustard

1 teaspoon Worcestershire
  sauce
¼ teaspoon cayenne pepper
¼ teaspoon fennel seed
½ cup heavy (whipping)
  cream
24 raw oysters in their shells
½ cup grated Parmesan
  cheese

1. Preheat the oven to 375°F.
2. In a medium saucepan over medium-high heat, melt the butter. Sauté the onion, celery, and garlic until soft and translucent, about 5 minutes. Stir in the spinach until well blended. Add the liqueur and cook for about 1 minute, allowing the liquid to evaporate.
3. Stir in the mustard, Worcestershire sauce, cayenne pepper, and fennel seed. Add the cream and simmer for about 5 minutes, stirring often, until thickened. Set the sauce aside.
4. Shuck the oysters, discarding the top shells. Place them on a baking sheet in their half-shells. Spoon the spinach mixture evenly over the oysters, then sprinkle with the Parmesan cheese. Bake for about 20 minutes, until browned and bubbling.
5. Transfer the oysters to a serving platter and serve with cocktail forks.

Thai-Style Shrimp Summer Rolls

SERVES 4

PREP TIME:
25 minutes

A balance of cooked and raw, sweet and sour, and hot and cold, summer rolls can be filled with just about any combination of protein, herbs, and vegetables.

FOR THE DIPPING SAUCE

1 tablespoon fish sauce
2 teaspoons sugar
2 teaspoons freshly squeezed
   lime juice

1 teaspoon peeled and grated
   fresh ginger
1 small Thai bird chile, roughly
   chopped (optional)
1 teaspoon water, if needed

FOR THE ROLLS

2 cups warm water
12 (8-inch) rice paper rounds
6 red leaf lettuce leaves,
   shredded
½ pound cooked rice
   vermicelli, drained and
   rinsed

½ cup shredded carrots
½ cup fresh mint leaves
½ cup fresh Thai basil leaves
12 large (U31/40) cooked
   shrimp, tail-off, peeled,
   deveined, and halved
   lengthwise

TO MAKE THE DIPPING SAUCE

1. In a small bowl, stir together the fish sauce, sugar, lime juice, ginger, and chile (if using). Taste and add water to thin out the sauce if needed.

TO MAKE THE ROLLS

2. Pour the warm water into a pie plate or shallow baking dish and dip the rice paper in the water one sheet at a time, then lay the sheets on a cutting board. Wait a few seconds for the rice paper to soften and become pliable.

3. Place a bit of lettuce, rice vermicelli, carrots, mint, Thai basil, and shrimp on the bottom third of a sheet of rice paper, making sure to place the shrimp in the center. Fold the bottom edge over the ingredients, then fold in the sides. Roll away from you into a tight, compact tube. Set the roll aside on a serving platter and repeat until you have 12 rolls.

4. To serve, slice each roll in half and arrange on a platter with the dipping sauce on the side.

TIP

Serve immediately or cover and set aside for up to 2 hours. Do not refrigerate, or the rice paper will become hard.

Salt Cod and Yukon Gold Croquettes

SERVES 6

PREP TIME:
5 minutes,
plus 12 hours
to chill

COOK TIME:
45 minutes,
plus
30 minutes
to chill

These crispy bites are a Portuguese street food classic, as is their key ingredient, salt cod or **bacalhau.** *This iteration features lots of herbs and lemon, a touch of briny capers, creamy Yukon Gold potatoes, and a bright, spicy sauce.*

1 pound boned salt cod fillets
1 pound Yukon Gold potatoes, peeled and cut into 1-inch chunks
Kosher salt
2 tablespoons extra-virgin olive oil
1 small yellow onion, finely diced
3 garlic cloves, minced
1 teaspoon red pepper flakes
¼ cup chopped fresh parsley
2 tablespoons chopped fresh thyme
Zest of 1 lemon, divided

2 tablespoons freshly squeezed lemon juice, divided
2 tablespoons capers, chopped, divided
1 tablespoon minced chives
1 tablespoon crème fraîche
Freshly ground black pepper
2 large eggs, beaten
1 cup bread crumbs
Avocado oil, for frying
1 cup mayonnaise
½ teaspoon sriracha
1 lemon, cut into wedges

1. Place the cod in a medium bowl and cover it with cold water. Cover with plastic wrap and refrigerate for 12 hours, changing the water halfway through.

2. Place the potatoes in a large pot and cover them with cold water. Generously season with salt and cook until fork-tender, about 15 minutes. Drain the potatoes, transfer them to a large bowl, and mash them thoroughly with a potato masher. Set aside.

3. Thoroughly rinse the cod and place it in a large saucepan with enough cold water to cover the fish. Bring to a boil over high heat, reduce the heat to low, and simmer for 5 minutes. Drain and rinse again. Transfer the cod to a baking sheet lined with a kitchen towel. Roll the cod back and forth over the towel until finely flaked.

4. In a large skillet over medium-high heat, heat the olive oil. Add the onion, garlic, and red pepper flakes and sauté until translucent, about 3 minutes. Stir in the cod and transfer the mixture to the bowl of potatoes. Add the parsley, thyme, half of the lemon zest, 1 tablespoon of lemon juice, 1 tablespoon of capers, the chives, and crème fraîche and mix to combine. Season with salt and pepper to taste. Add the eggs and mix to combine.

5. Line a large baking sheet with parchment paper. Pour the bread crumbs into a medium shallow dish and season with salt and pepper. Form the cod mixture into 1½-inch balls and roll them in the bread crumbs. Place them on the parchment-lined baking sheet and refrigerate for 30 minutes.

6. In a large Dutch oven over medium heat, heat 3 inches of avocado oil to 350°F. Working in batches, fry the croquettes for 1 to 2 minutes, until golden brown, turning occasionally. Transfer them to a paper towel–lined baking sheet. Feel free to keep the croquettes warm on a baking sheet in a 275°F oven while frying the remaining ones.

7. In a small bowl, mix the mayonnaise, the remaining lemon zest, the remaining 1 tablespoon of lemon juice, the remaining 1 tablespoon of capers, and the sriracha. Taste and adjust the seasoning, if needed. Serve the croquettes with the sauce and lemon wedges.

Lemony Baked Crab Dip

SERVES 4

PREP TIME:
15 minutes

COOK TIME:
20 minutes

This dip has a hint of spice, umami-rich Parmigiano, fresh herbs, and plenty of lemony goodness. Serve alongside crusty bread or your favorite crackers or chips.

4 ounces cream cheese, at room temperature
¼ cup mayonnaise
¼ cup crème fraîche
1 red serrano or Fresno chile, seeded, pith removed, and finely diced
2 garlic cloves, minced
2 teaspoons lemon zest
¼ teaspoon Old Bay seasoning
¼ cup parsley, roughly chopped
8 ounces fresh lump crabmeat

¾ cup grated Parmigiano-Reggiano cheese, divided
½ cup shredded white cheddar cheese, divided
6 scallions, white and green parts, thinly sliced
2 tablespoons freshly squeezed lemon juice
Kosher salt
Freshly ground black pepper
16 Ritz crackers, crushed into fine crumbs
Lemon wedges, for serving

1. Preheat the oven to 325°F.
2. In a medium mixing bowl, mix the cream cheese, mayonnaise, and crème fraîche. Add the serrano, garlic, lemon zest, Old Bay seasoning, and parsley. Stir to combine. Add the crab, half of the Parmigiano-Reggiano cheese, ¼ cup of cheddar cheese, the scallions, and lemon juice and gently fold to combine. Season with salt and pepper to taste.
3. Transfer the dip to a lightly greased 8-by-8-inch casserole dish. Top the dip with the remaining Parmigiano-Reggiano and remaining ¼ cup of cheddar, followed by the cracker crumbs. Bake until bubbly and golden brown, about 20 minutes. Serve with the lemon wedges.

3

SALADS & HANDHELDS

TIP

Swap in salmon for the tuna; this would also be a great recipe for using up leftover grilled fish or shrimp.

Heirloom Tomato and Tuna Panzanella

SERVES 6

PREP TIME:
15 minutes

COOK TIME:
10 minutes

One of the beautiful things about panzanella is that you can switch it up based on the produce you have on hand.

½ cup extra-virgin olive oil,
   plus 3 tablespoons
1 loaf crusty French bread,
   cut into 1-inch cubes (about
   6 cups)
Kosher salt
Freshly ground black pepper
1 garlic clove, minced
3 tablespoons white wine
   vinegar
1 teaspoon Dijon mustard

½ teaspoon honey
2 large heirloom tomatoes,
   cut into 1-inch cubes
1 English cucumber, seeded
   and cut into 1-inch cubes
½ red onion, thinly sliced
8 to 10 basil leaves, torn
¼ cup Niçoise or kalamata
   olives, pitted and chopped
2 (6-ounce) cans oil-packed
   tuna, drained

1. Line a baking sheet with paper towels.
2. In a large skillet over medium-low heat, heat 3 tablespoons of olive oil. Add the bread cubes, season with salt and pepper, and cook, tossing frequently, until nicely browned, about 10 minutes. Reduce the heat to low if the bread starts to brown too quickly. Transfer the cubes to the lined baking sheet.
3. In a small bowl, whisk together the garlic, vinegar, Dijon mustard, and honey. While still whisking, stream in the remaining ½ cup of olive oil until emulsified. Season with salt and pepper.
4. In a large salad bowl, combine the tomatoes, cucumber, onion, basil, and olives. Add the bread and toss. Gently flake in the tuna and add the vinaigrette, tossing to combine.
5. Serve or store the components separately (toasted bread, salad, and dressing) for up to 2 days in the refrigerator.

Pistachio-Crusted Tuna and Lentil Salad

SERVES 4

PREP TIME:
15 minutes

COOK TIME:
35 minutes

Lemony lentil salad studded with scallions and lightly laced with a hint of curry makes a delicious foundation for rich tuna encrusted in buttery pistachios.

2 cups low-sodium vegetable broth

1 cup Puy lentils

1 bay leaf

2 medium carrots, peeled and coarsely grated

2 scallions, white and green parts, thinly sliced

1 cup grape tomatoes, halved

Zest and juice of 1 lemon

½ cup extra-virgin olive oil

1 tablespoon red wine vinegar

1 tablespoon curry powder

Kosher salt

Freshly ground black pepper

1 cup shelled pistachios

2 tablespoons all-purpose flour

4 (4- to 5-ounce) tuna steaks

2 tablespoons grapeseed oil or canola oil

1. In a medium saucepan over medium heat, combine the broth, lentils, and bay leaf. Add water to cover by 2 inches. Bring to a boil, reduce the heat to low, and simmer until the lentils are tender but still firm, 20 to 25 minutes. Drain and discard the bay leaf. Transfer the lentils to a medium bowl and set aside to cool.

2. Once cooled slightly, stir in the carrots, scallions, tomatoes, and lemon zest. Stir in the lemon juice, olive oil, vinegar, and curry powder and season with salt and pepper. Set aside.

3. In a food processor, pulse the pistachios until finely chopped. Transfer to a wide, shallow dish and stir in the flour. Season each side of the tuna with salt and pepper, then dredge the tuna in the pistachio mixture.

4. In a large nonstick skillet over medium-high heat, heat the grapeseed oil. When the oil begins to smoke, sear the tuna for 7 to 8 minutes, flipping halfway through. Both sides should be brown and crispy, but the center should be medium-rare. The fish is done when an instant-read digital thermometer reads 130°F. Transfer to a warmed plate and tent with foil for 10 minutes.

5. Thinly slice the tuna. Serve atop the lentil salad.

TIP

Salmon makes a great alternative in this salad if tuna isn't available.

Anchovy, Kale, and Salmon Caesar Salad with Lemony Bread Crumbs

SERVES 4

PREP TIME:
10 minutes

COOK TIME:
20 minutes

Feel free to swap the kale for romaine or whatever fresh greens you have in your produce drawer. The dressing is also delicious for topping fish before roasting or grilling.

1 pound salmon
Kosher salt
Freshly ground black pepper
6 tablespoons lemon juice, divided
½ cup extra-virgin olive oil, plus 2 tablespoons, plus more for drizzling
3 or 4 anchovies or 3 inches anchovy paste

1 garlic clove, minced
1½ tablespoons Dijon mustard
⅓ cup grated Parmigiano-Reggiano cheese
1½ cups panko bread crumbs
Zest of 1 lemon
1 bunch kale (about 6 cups), ribs removed

1. Preheat the oven to 425°F. Line a baking sheet with parchment paper.

2. Season the salmon with salt and pepper. In a small bowl, whisk 3 tablespoons of lemon juice and stream in 2 tablespoons of olive oil until emulsified. Season with salt and pepper. Place the salmon on the baking sheet and pour the dressing over the salmon. Bake until it reaches an internal temperature of 145°F, 15 to 20 minutes.

3. While the salmon is cooking, in a small bowl, mash the anchovies with the garlic. Whisk in the remaining 3 tablespoons of lemon juice and the Dijon mustard. While still whisking, drizzle in the remaining ½ cup of olive oil, then add the cheese. Season with salt and pepper. Set aside.

4. In a large skillet over medium-low heat, heat a drizzle of oil. Add the bread crumbs and lemon zest. Toss until golden brown, about 3 minutes.

5. Tear the kale leaves into bite-size pieces and put them in a large bowl. Massage a little of the anchovy dressing into the leaves to tenderize the kale.

6. Add three-quarters of the bread crumbs and the rest of the anchovy dressing to the kale and toss to combine. Plate the kale, top with the salmon, and sprinkle with the remaining bread crumbs. Serve.

TIP

Make the dressing up to 3 days in advance and store it in an airtight container.

Tuna Niçoise Salad

SERVES 4

PREP TIME:
10 minutes

There's always been a debate over what is a "correct" Niçoise salad. To the purists, it's clear: no vinegar, no lettuce, no fresh tuna, and absolutely no boiled vegetables, like potatoes or green beans. This recipe is a purist version, but feel free to make any adjustments you'd like.

4 ripe tomatoes, sliced
Sea salt
Freshly ground black pepper
1 green bell pepper, seeded
  and cut into thin strips
8 radishes, trimmed and
  thinly sliced into rounds
1 English cucumber, peeled
  and thinly sliced into rounds
8 oil-packed canned
  anchovies

8 ounces oil-packed canned
  tuna
½ cup pitted Niçoise or
  kalamata olives
10 fresh basil leaves,
  shredded
4 hard-boiled eggs, peeled
  and halved
¼ cup extra-virgin olive oil

1. Arrange the tomatoes on a large platter and season with salt and pepper to taste.

2. Add the bell pepper, radishes, cucumber, anchovies, tuna with the oil, olives, and basil in that order. Arrange the hard-boiled eggs around the salad and drizzle the whole platter with the olive oil.

TIP

For some variation, add any combination of the following to the traditional base: 2 romaine hearts, bottoms trimmed and separated into leaves; 8 small potatoes, boiled until tender and cooled; 24 green beans, blanched until crisp-tender and cooled; 1 cup of chopped celery; ½ cup of fresh-cooked or canned fava beans; and 1 cup of fresh-cooked or canned baby artichokes cut in half.

Mason Jar Sushi Salad

SERVES 4

PREP TIME:
15 minutes

COOK TIME:
45 minutes

Enjoy sushi at home without having to learn how to craft the perfect sushi roll. Putting the dressing in the bottom of the jar keeps the salad contents from getting soggy.

TIP

To save time on prep work, use a store-bought ginger dressing.

FOR THE GINGER DRESSING

½ cup finely chopped yellow onion
¼ cup shredded carrots
¼ cup rice vinegar
2½ tablespoons peeled and minced ginger

2 tablespoons water
1½ tablespoons honey
1 tablespoon low-sodium soy sauce
1 teaspoon hot chili sauce
½ teaspoon minced garlic

FOR THE SUSHI SALAD

2 cups water
1 cup short-grain brown rice
1 cup shelled edamame, fresh or frozen and thawed
1 cup julienned cucumber

1 cup shredded carrots
6 ounces crabmeat or sushi-grade fish
2 seaweed sheets, crumbled or cut into thin strips

TO MAKE THE GINGER DRESSING

1. In a blender or food processor, blend the onion, carrots, rice vinegar, ginger, water, honey, soy sauce, chili sauce, and garlic until mostly smooth. Set it aside.

TIP

You can also make this salad gluten-free by using coconut aminos instead of soy sauce.

TO MAKE THE SUSHI SALAD

2. In a medium saucepan, combine the water and the rice and bring to a boil over high heat. Reduce the heat to low, cover, and simmer for 45 minutes. Allow the rice to cool slightly before assembling the jars.

3. Divide the dressing among four Mason jars. Layer in the rice, edamame, cucumber, carrots, and crabmeat. Garnish with the crumbled seaweed. Shake the jars before eating.

Tilapia Tacos with Cabbage Slaw

SERVES 4

PREP TIME:
10 minutes

COOK TIME:
20 minutes

Tilapia is excellent for fish tacos because it's sturdy enough to maintain its structure.

½ head green cabbage, finely shredded

½ small red onion, cut into ¼-inch dice

¼ cup loosely packed fresh cilantro leaves

1 small jalapeño pepper, seeded and minced

Kosher salt

Freshly ground black pepper

2 tablespoons sour cream or Mexican crema

1 tablespoon freshly squeezed lime juice

2 (½-pound) tilapia fillets, each cut into 4 equal pieces

1 teaspoon ground cumin

½ teaspoon chili powder

3 tablespoons avocado oil

16 (6-inch) corn tortillas

2 limes, quartered, for garnish

1. In a small bowl, toss together the cabbage, onion, cilantro, and jalapeño. Season with salt and pepper. Toss with the sour cream and lime juice, cover, and refrigerate until ready to serve.

2. Heat a cast-iron skillet over medium-high heat. While the pan is heating, season both sides of the fish with the cumin, chili powder, salt, and pepper.

3. Heat the oil in the skillet until it reaches its smoke point. Add the fish and sear on each side for 4 minutes, flipping halfway through. Transfer the fish to a clean plate and tent with aluminum foil.

4. Wipe out the skillet with dry paper towels and return it to medium-high heat. Toast the tortillas, two at a time, for 1 minute each, flipping halfway through.

5. To assemble, break the fish into small chunks and arrange the chunks on top of 8 double stacks of tortillas. Lightly season each taco with salt and pepper and a squeeze of juice from the limes. Top with the cabbage slaw. Serve immediately.

Quick and Easy Oyster Po'Boys

**SERVES
2 TO 4**

PREP TIME:
15 minutes

COOK TIME:
20 minutes

This recipe covers all the bases for a classic fried oyster po'boy but is simplified without the fuss of deep-frying. If you don't like oysters, consider swapping them for shrimp or a catfish fillet instead.

FOR THE OYSTERS

3 tablespoons avocado oil
6 to 8 fresh oysters, shucked
Kosher salt
Freshly ground black pepper

2 cups all-purpose flour, plus
   more if needed
1 large egg, beaten
2 cups panko bread crumbs

FOR THE SANDWICH

3 tablespoons mayonnaise
2 teaspoons prepared
   horseradish
1 teaspoon Creole seasoning
1 teaspoon freshly squeezed
   lemon juice
Kosher salt

Freshly ground black pepper
2 French sandwich rolls, split
   in half
2 ripe Roma tomatoes, cut
   into ¼-inch-thick slices
2 or 3 green leaf lettuce leaves

TO MAKE THE OYSTERS

1. In a large nonstick skillet, heat the oil over medium-high heat. While the skillet is heating, pat the oysters dry with a paper towel and season both sides with salt and pepper. Put the flour, beaten egg, and bread crumbs in three separate bowls.

2. Take one oyster, coat it with flour, dip it in the beaten egg, then coat it with bread crumbs. Repeat with the remaining oysters, then place them in the skillet, working in batches so as not to overcrowd the skillet. Fry the oysters until golden brown on both sides, flipping halfway through, 6 to 7 minutes in total. Transfer to a paper towel–lined plate.

TO ASSEMBLE THE SANDWICH

3. Preheat the oven to broil. Line a baking sheet with aluminum foil.

4. In a small bowl, mix the mayonnaise, horseradish, Creole seasoning, and lemon juice, and season with salt and pepper.

5. Toast the bread slightly by broiling it for a few seconds. Transfer the rolls to warmed plates and spread the mayonnaise mixture on one side of each roll. Evenly divide the oysters among the rolls and top with the sliced tomatoes and lettuce.

TIP

Fresh oysters from a jar will do just fine for this sandwich.

Pan Bagnat (Provençal Tuna Sandwiches)

SERVES 4

PREP TIME:
20 minutes,
plus
10 minutes
to chill

Part tuna sandwich and part tuna Niçoise salad, this is a cousin to the Italian muffuletta sandwich.

¼ cup store-bought olive tapenade spread

1 small garlic clove, minced

1 small shallot, minced

2 oil-packed canned anchovy fillets, finely chopped

1 cup coarsely chopped fresh parsley leaves

1 tablespoon red wine vinegar

1 tablespoon Dijon mustard

3 tablespoons extra-virgin olive oil, divided

1 (5-ounce) can oil-packed tuna, drained and oil reserved

1 French baguette, split lengthwise and lightly toasted

2 large soft-boiled eggs, peeled and thinly sliced

1 large Roma tomato, sliced into ¼-inch-thick rounds

2 roasted red peppers from a jar, sliced into thin strips

Freshly ground black pepper

1. In a small bowl, mix the tapenade, garlic, shallot, anchovies, and parsley. Stir in the red wine vinegar and Dijon mustard. Drizzle in 1 tablespoon of olive oil and stir to combine.

2. Drizzle 2 teaspoons of the reserved tuna oil over each side of the baguette. Spread both sides of the bread with the tapenade mixture. Top with the tuna, add alternating slices of the eggs and tomato, and top with the red peppers. Drizzle the remaining 2 tablespoons of olive oil over the top and season with pepper.

3. Wrap the sandwich tightly in foil and cut it in half. Wrap in another piece of foil or plastic wrap and place the halves side by side. Weigh the sandwiches down with something heavy. Refrigerate for 10 to 15 minutes.

4. Unwrap the sandwiches and cut them in half again to serve.

TIP

Any leftover finfish you have from another recipe will work beautifully in this sandwich.

Trout Hand Pies

SERVES 4

PREP TIME:
1 hour

COOK TIME:
1 hour
20 minutes,
plus
20 minutes
to cool

Like empanadas, these savory pies are extra tasty and make a great lunch paired with a salad. This recipe is a little time-consuming, but have faith. The frozen puff pastry will save you some time.

FOR THE FILLING

1 small russet potato, peeled and cut into 2-inch cubes

6 tablespoons (¾ stick) unsalted butter, at room temperature

1 small shallot, minced

1 pound trout fillets, skinned, pin bones removed, and cut into 2-inch chunks

Kosher salt

Freshly ground black pepper

2 tablespoons sour cream

1 tablespoon finely chopped fresh parsley

1 tablespoon finely chopped fresh dill

Zest and juice of 1 lemon

1 large egg white

FOR THE PUFF PASTRY

1 (17-ounce) package frozen puff pastry, thawed in the refrigerator

¼ cup all-purpose flour, for dusting

1 large egg, beaten with 1 teaspoon water

½ tablespoon flaky sea salt

TO MAKE THE FILLING

1. Place the potato cubes in a small pot and cover with cold water by 1 inch. Bring to a boil over high heat and cook until fork-tender, 15 to 20 minutes. Drain the potatoes and return them to the pot to allow excess moisture to evaporate. Cut the potatoes into ½-inch chunks.

2. In a large nonstick skillet over medium heat, melt the butter and sauté the shallot until translucent, about 4 minutes. While the shallot is cooking, lightly season the trout with salt and

pepper. Cook half of the trout pieces, about 6 minutes, flipping halfway through. Put the cooked fish in a large bowl and cook the remaining fish. Transfer all the butter, shallots, and fish to the bowl and cool the fish to room temperature.

3. When the fish is cool, flake it with a fork until you have random-size chunks and flakes. Stir in the cooked potatoes, sour cream, parsley, dill, lemon zest, and lemon juice. Season with salt and pepper and stir to combine; the mixture should be thick and paste-like.

4. In a small bowl, whisk the egg white until foamy and fold it into the fish mixture. Cover and refrigerate for about 30 minutes.

TO MAKE THE PUFF PASTRY

5. Preheat the oven to 400°F and line a baking sheet with parchment paper.

6. Remove the puff pastry from the refrigerator. Dust a clean work surface and rolling pin with a bit of flour and roll one sheet of puff pastry out to a roughly 12-by-16-inch rectangle. Cut the pastry in half to create two pieces that are each about 8 by 12 inches. Repeat this process with the second sheet of pastry. Fold each piece in half like a book to make a crease, then unfold.

7. Divide the filling among the pieces, placing each portion in the center of the right side of each piece of pastry. Spread the filling slightly, leaving a ½-inch edge around the perimeter. Fold the left side of the pastry over the filling and line up the edges. Use a fork to crimp the edges around the pastry and place the pies on the prepared baking sheet.

8. Brush the tops of the pies with the beaten egg and sprinkle with a small pinch of salt. Cut two 1-inch-long slits on the top of

Continued on next page ⟶

each pie. Wrap the pies in plastic wrap and chill in the freezer for 20 minutes, or until the pastry feels firm.

9. Remove the pies from the freezer and discard the plastic wrap. Bake until golden brown, about 35 to 40 minutes. Transfer the pies to a wire cooling rack and cool for at least 20 minutes. Serve warm.

TIP

For the flakiest crust, refrigerate the assembled pies overnight before baking them. You can also use cooked salmon, tuna, or catfish in place of the trout. Canned, fresh, or even leftover fish works great for the filling!

Cornmeal-Crusted Catfish Sandwiches

SERVES 6

PREP TIME:
15 minutes

COOK TIME:
25 minutes

This Southern staple gets paired with an herbaceous, garlicky buttermilk ranch dressing, crunchy slaw, red onion, and creamy avocado—all in a brioche bun.

1 cup mayonnaise

½ cup sour cream

2 garlic cloves, minced

2 tablespoons chopped fresh dill

2 tablespoons minced chives

½ tablespoon lemon zest

½ tablespoon freshly squeezed lemon juice

¼ teaspoon Worcestershire sauce

Kosher salt

Freshly ground black pepper

3½ cups buttermilk, divided

2 cups shredded purple cabbage

Avocado oil, for frying

1½ pounds catfish fillets

1 cup all-purpose flour

1½ cups cornmeal

6 brioche buns, lightly toasted

1 avocado, peeled, pitted, and thinly sliced

1 red onion, thinly sliced

1. In a small bowl, combine the mayonnaise, sour cream, garlic, dill, chives, lemon zest, lemon juice, Worcestershire sauce, and a pinch of salt and black pepper and whisk to combine. While whisking, pour in up to ½ cup of buttermilk until the dressing reaches your desired consistency. Season to taste. Cover and refrigerate.

2. In a medium bowl, combine the cabbage with 1 tablespoon of dressing. Season with salt and pepper and toss thoroughly to combine. Cover and refrigerate.

3. In a large Dutch oven over medium heat, heat 4 inches of avocado oil to 350°F.

Continued on next page ⟶

4. Line a baking sheet with paper towels and set a wire rack on top.

5. Season the catfish with salt and pepper. If the fillets are wider than 3 inches, halve them lengthwise. Place the flour and cornmeal in two separate shallow dishes, seasoning each with a pinch of salt and pepper. Pour the remaining 3 cups of buttermilk into another large bowl. Dredge the fillets in the flour (shaking off any excess), then dip them in the buttermilk and then in the cornmeal. Use your hands to press the cornmeal into the fillets so it adheres, and shake off any excess. Place the breaded catfish on an unlined baking sheet.

6. Fry the fish in batches, 2 or 3 at a time, until golden brown, 2 minutes per side. Cool for 5 minutes before assembling.

7. Assemble each sandwich by swiping some buttermilk ranch on the bottom bun, then adding the avocado slices, catfish fillets, cabbage slaw, and red onion. Top with the other bun half and serve.

TIP

Shrimp is a great substitution in this twist on a classic.

Smoked Salmon and Orzo Salad

SERVES 4

PREP TIME:
15 minutes

COOK TIME:
10 minutes

A perfect side or main dish, orzo salad is truly a wonder. Smoked salmon makes a delicious protein addition.

½ cup extra-virgin olive oil, plus more for oiling the baking sheet
1½ cups dried orzo
¼ cup lemon juice
Zest of 1 lemon
1 large garlic clove, minced
1 teaspoon Dijon mustard
Kosher salt

Freshly ground black pepper
4 ounces hot smoked salmon
¼ cup pine nuts
1 English cucumber, diced
1 cup cherry tomatoes, halved
4 scallions, white and green parts, sliced
¼ cup chopped fresh basil

1. Bring a large pot of salted water to a boil over high heat and lightly oil a large, rimmed baking sheet. Cook the orzo until al dente, about 7 to 8 minutes. Drain and immediately transfer to the prepared baking sheet. Cool the orzo in the refrigerator.

2. In a liquid measuring cup, combine the lemon juice, lemon zest, garlic, mustard, and a pinch of salt and pepper. While whisking, slowly stream in the olive oil, a little at a time until the vinaigrette is fully emulsified. Season with additional salt as desired.

3. Flake the salmon into large chunks.

4. Toast the pine nuts in a dry sauté pan over medium-low heat, stirring regularly, until you begin to smell their nuttiness and they are golden brown, about 2 minutes.

5. Transfer the orzo to a large bowl and combine it with the cucumbers, tomatoes, pine nuts, scallions, and basil. Pour some of the vinaigrette over the orzo and toss to combine. Add the salmon and more vinaigrette as desired, and season with salt and pepper to taste.

TIP

This is delicious with everything from the tomatoes featured here to roasted veggies like broccoli, eggplant, and sun-dried tomatoes.

Crab Louie Salad

SERVES 4

PREP TIME:
15 minutes

COOK TIME:
20 minutes

The bright and creamy dressing for this salad is studded with briny capers, the perfect foil to the sweet crabmeat.

8 bacon slices

8 asparagus spears, woody ends removed

½ cup mayonnaise

Zest of 1 lemon

2½ tablespoons capers, drained, divided

1 tablespoon Dijon mustard

½ tablespoon freshly squeezed lemon juice

1 teaspoon apple cider vinegar

1 teaspoon Worcestershire sauce

1 large garlic clove, minced

Kosher salt

Freshly ground black pepper

1 medium head romaine lettuce, torn

1 English cucumber, diced

1 cup cherry tomatoes, halved

4 scallions, white and green parts, thinly sliced

1 large avocado, peeled, pitted, and sliced

8 ounces cooked crabmeat

1. Preheat the oven to 400°F. Arrange the bacon in an even layer on a large baking sheet and cook until crispy, about 20 minutes.

2. Bring a large pot of salted water to a rolling boil and prepare an ice bath in a large bowl. Add the asparagus and cook for about 2 to 3 minutes, depending on the size of the spears, until bright green and crisp-tender. Transfer to the ice bath.

3. In a small bowl, mix the mayonnaise, lemon zest, 1 tablespoon of capers, Dijon mustard, lemon juice, vinegar, Worcestershire sauce, and garlic. Season with salt and pepper.

4. Arrange the lettuce on a large platter. Top with the cucumber, tomatoes, scallions, remaining 1½ tablespoons of capers, asparagus, and avocado. Top with the crab and pour the dressing over everything. Break the bacon into small pieces and sprinkle over the salad. Serve.

Salmon Burgers

SERVES 4

PREP TIME:
20 minutes,
plus 1 hour
to chill

COOK TIME:
15 minutes

With a crisp exterior, an equally light interior, and notes of lemon and alliums, these salmon cakes are a cut above the rest.

1¼ pounds salmon fillets, skinned and pin bones removed

1 cup mayonnaise, plus 1½ tablespoons

1½ tablespoons Dijon mustard

2½ teaspoons lemon zest, divided

2 tablespoons freshly squeezed lemon juice, plus 1 teaspoon

1 teaspoon Worcestershire sauce

1 cup panko bread crumbs, plus 2½ tablespoons

3 scallions, white and green parts, sliced

2 tablespoons chopped fresh parsley

Kosher salt

Freshly ground black pepper

2½ tablespoons extra-virgin olive oil, plus more for brushing

1 tablespoon soy sauce

1 teaspoon miso paste

4 brioche buns, halved and lightly toasted

4 large romaine lettuce leaves

1 avocado, peeled, pitted, and sliced

½ red onion, sliced

1. Cut three-quarters of the salmon into ¼-inch pieces. Cut the remaining salmon into larger chunks and transfer them to a food processor, along with 1½ tablespoons of mayonnaise, the Dijon mustard, 1½ teaspoons of lemon zest, 2 tablespoons of lemon juice, and the Worcestershire sauce. Pulse until a rough paste forms. Transfer the mixture to a large bowl along with the reserved salmon pieces, 2½ tablespoons of bread crumbs, the scallions, parsley, and a pinch of salt and pepper. Mix to combine.

Continued on next page ⟶

2. Line a large baking sheet with parchment paper and brush with olive oil or spray with nonstick cooking spray. Using moist hands, form the salmon mixture into 4 (4-inch-wide and ¾-inch-thick) patties. Place the patties on the prepared baking sheet, cover, and refrigerate for 1 hour.

3. Place the remaining 1 cup of bread crumbs in a shallow dish and press each side of the salmon burgers into the bread crumbs.

4. In a medium bowl, mix the remaining 1 cup of mayonnaise, remaining 1 teaspoon of lemon zest, remaining 1 teaspoon of lemon juice, the soy sauce, and miso. Refrigerate until ready to serve.

5. In a large skillet over medium-high heat, heat the olive oil. Carefully add the patties, working in batches so as not to overcrowd the pan, and cook until golden brown on the bottom, 3 to 4 minutes per side. Transfer to a paper towel–lined baking sheet and season with a sprinkle of salt.

6. Top the buns with the sauce, salmon patties, lettuce, avocado, and red onion.

7. Store leftover patties in an airtight container in the refrigerator for up to 2 days. Alternatively, place the salmon patties in a freezer bag between sheets of parchment paper and freeze for up to 2 months.

Grilled Mahi-Mahi Tacos

SERVES 4

PREP TIME:
30 minutes

COOK TIME:
15 minutes

Here, mahi-mahi gets topped with a creamy, slightly spicy, cilantro-forward sauce and bright, juicy, crunchy mango slaw. Serve with lime wedges and, preferably, a beer.

1 avocado, peeled and pitted
2 cups roughly chopped cilantro, plus 2 tablespoons
¼ cup lime juice, plus 2 tablespoons
2 serrano peppers, seeded, pith removed, and diced, divided
2 garlic cloves, minced
½ tablespoon sour cream
¼ cup olive oil, plus 1 tablespoon
Kosher salt

Freshly ground black pepper
1 mango, peeled, pitted, and cut into ¼-inch dice
1 cup thinly sliced purple cabbage
½ red onion, sliced
4 (5- to 6-ounce) mahi-mahi fillets
Avocado oil, for brushing
8 (6-inch) flour tortillas
Lime wedges, for serving
Hot sauce, for serving

1. In a food processor, combine the avocado, 2 cups of cilantro, ¼ cup of lime juice, half of the serrano peppers, the garlic, and sour cream. Pulse to combine, then pause and scrape down the bowl. Pulse again, and while processing, stream in ¼ cup of olive oil and blend until smooth and fluffy. Season with salt and pepper to taste. Refrigerate until ready to serve.

2. In a large bowl, toss the mango, cabbage, red onion, the remaining 2 tablespoons of cilantro, the remaining 2 tablespoons of lime juice, the remaining serrano peppers, and the remaining 1 tablespoon of olive oil. Season with salt and pepper to taste. Refrigerate until ready to serve.

Continued on next page ⟶

3. Prepare an outdoor grill and bring the temperature to medium-high heat (400°F to 450°F). Brush the mahi-mahi fillets all over with avocado oil and season with salt and pepper. Grill the fillets, round-side down, until you can lift the fish off of the grates without it sticking, about 5 minutes per side. Cover with foil and let rest for 10 minutes. Alternatively, place a grill pan over medium heat and brush with avocado oil. Place the fillets on the pan and cook 3 to 4 minutes per side, until the fish flakes easily.

4. Grill the tortillas until some slight char develops on each side, about 20 to 30 seconds per side. Flake the fish into large pieces. Divide the mahi-mahi among the tortillas and top each with the mango slaw and the avocado-cilantro sauce. Serve with lime wedges and hot sauce.

Crispy Tilapia Tacos

SERVES 4

PREP TIME:
30 minutes

COOK TIME:
15 minutes

There are a few requirements for a taco to be Baja-style: the fish must be crispy, and there must be a tangy white sauce, cabbage, plenty of lime, and corn tortillas. I don't make the rules, but in this case, they're delicious.

¾ cup sour cream
¼ cup mayonnaise
1½ teaspoons lime zest
1 large garlic clove, minced
1 teaspoon sriracha
Kosher salt
½ teaspoon freshly ground black pepper, plus more for seasoning
2 tablespoons lime juice
Avocado oil, for frying
1¼ cups all-purpose flour

¼ cup cornstarch
1 teaspoon salt
½ teaspoon chili powder
1¼ cups Mexican beer
2 pounds tilapia fillets, halved widthwise
8 (6-inch) corn tortillas
2 cups sliced cabbage
1 avocado, peeled, pitted, and sliced
½ red onion, sliced
Lime wedges, for serving

1. In a small bowl, whisk together the sour cream, mayonnaise, lime zest, garlic, and sriracha, along with a pinch of kosher salt and pepper. Whisk in the lime juice. Cover with plastic wrap and refrigerate until ready to serve.

2. In a large Dutch oven over medium heat, heat 3 inches of avocado oil to 350°F.

3. In a large bowl, whisk together the flour, cornstarch, salt, chili powder, and ½ teaspoon of pepper. Slowly pour in the beer while whisking.

Continued on next page ⟶

4. Season the tilapia with kosher salt and pepper, dip the fillets in the batter, shaking off any excess, and carefully place into the oil, frying in batches, 2 to 3 minutes per side, until golden brown. Transfer to a paper towel–lined baking sheet.

5. Grill the tortillas in a large skillet over medium-high heat for about 1 minute each. Assemble the tacos with the garlicky white sauce, cabbage, avocado, and red onion. Serve with lime wedges.

TIP

Feel free to substitute another thin fillet, like catfish, for the tilapia.

White Clam Pizza

SERVES 2

PREP TIME:
1 hour
30 minutes

COOK TIME:
20 minutes

This take on a New Haven, Connecticut, classic features a flavorful, creamy clam cooking liquid as its base. Lots of chopped fresh littleneck clams and plenty of Parmigiano-Reggiano cheese make this a delicious dish.

24 littleneck clams, scrubbed
2 tablespoons extra-virgin olive oil
1 shallot, minced
¼ teaspoon red pepper flakes
7 garlic cloves, chopped
¼ cup chopped fresh parsley
3 thyme sprigs
1 cup white wine
Kosher salt

2 tablespoons heavy (whipping) cream
Pinch freshly ground black pepper
Cornmeal, for dusting
1 pound premade refrigerated pizza dough
1¼ cups grated Parmigiano-Reggiano cheese
Lemon wedges, for serving

1. Place the clams in a bowl of salted water for 30 minutes to purge them of any sand. Pick out the clams individually. Discard the water and rinse the bowl thoroughly before returning the clams to the bowl and soaking for 15 minutes more. Pick the clams out of the water individually when done.

2. In a large skillet over medium heat, heat the olive oil. Sauté the shallots and red pepper flakes for 30 seconds before adding the garlic, parsley, and thyme. Pour in the wine, then add the clams, stirring to coat. Season with salt. Cover, reduce the heat to low, and allow the clams to steam until opened, about 7 minutes. Discard any clams that don't open.

Continued on next page ⟶

3. Remove the clams from the cooking liquid, place them in another bowl, and set aside. Increase the heat to medium, add the cream to the cooking liquid, add the pepper, stir, and simmer until reduced slightly, about 5 minutes.

4. Once the clams are cool enough to handle, remove the meat from the shells and roughly chop before returning them to the bowl and tossing with 1 tablespoon of the cooking liquid.

5. Preheat the oven to 500°F. Dust a pizza peel and a pizza stone with cornmeal. Set the pizza stone on the middle rack of the oven. Stretch the pizza dough out into a 12-inch circle. Working very quickly, transfer the dough to the pizza peel and spread a layer of the cooking liquid on the dough, followed by a generous sprinkling of Parmigiano-Reggiano, chopped clams, and more Parmigiano-Reggiano.

6. Place the pizza peel in line with the stone in the oven. Use a swift motion to slide the pizza onto the stone. Bake for 8 minutes, or until golden brown. Let rest for 3 minutes before cutting.

7. Serve with lemon wedges.

TIP

Instead of a pizza stone, you can use a preheated large cast-iron skillet or a preheated large baking sheet—both dusted with cornmeal.

Sardine and Pimento Bocadillos

SERVES 4

PREP TIME:
10 minutes

COOK TIME:
5 minutes

The bocadillo is an iconic Spanish street food sandwich. This version of a bocadillo, made with sardines, is a spin on a Spanish tapa, pan con tomate—toasted baguette rubbed with garlic and tomato.

1 soft French baguette, split in half lengthwise
1 large garlic clove, peeled
1 small Roma tomato, halved
3 tablespoons extra-virgin olive oil
Kosher salt
Freshly ground black pepper
1 (4-ounce) can oil-packed sardines, oil reserved
1 (4-ounce) jar sliced pimentos, drained

1. Preheat the oven to broil. Line a baking sheet with foil.
2. Place the baguette, cut-side up, on the prepared baking sheet. Toast the bread under the broiler for 2 minutes, or until the surface is golden. Leave the oven on broil.
3. Lightly rub the garlic over the toasted surface and then follow with the tomato, pressing lightly to smear some of the tomato juices and pulp onto the bread. Save the garlic and tomato to use in another recipe or chop them up and eat them on toast with a bit of olive oil.
4. Drizzle the olive oil over the bread and season lightly with salt and pepper. Place the sardines on one side of the baguette, then top with the pimentos. Drizzle 1 or 2 teaspoons of the reserved sardine oil over the pimentos.
5. Broil the sandwich for another 2 to 3 minutes to heat the sardines and pimentos. Remove from the broiler and close the sandwich. Cut into 4 equal pieces and serve.

TIP

Use canned tuna or smoked mackerel instead of sardines.

4

SOUPS, STEWS, & CHOWDERS

Miso Whitefish Soup with Chard

SERVES 4

PREP TIME:
10 minutes

COOK TIME:
15 minutes

Miso soup is a traditional Japanese dish featuring a base broth combined with fermented soybeans. When the miso paste is mixed into the broth, it's called dashi. The type of miso paste you use defines the character and flavor of the soup, so pick the one you like the most. White miso paste is only briefly fermented, so it's sweeter and lighter making it a good choice if you've never cooked with miso. Red miso paste is fermented longer so its flavor is more pungent.

6 cups low-sodium vegetable stock

2 tablespoons white miso paste

1 tablespoon peeled and grated fresh ginger

1 pound whitefish, thinly sliced

2 cups roughly chopped Swiss chard, thoroughly washed

1. In a large saucepan, bring the vegetable stock to a boil over medium-high heat.
2. Stir in the miso paste and ginger and simmer for 5 minutes.
3. Add the whitefish and simmer until just cooked through, about 5 minutes.
4. Stir in the chard and simmer until wilted, about 3 minutes.
5. Serve immediately.

TIP

Miso paste is an incredibly versatile ingredient and can be used in many different preparations. Try making a savory miso salad dressing with ¼ cup of olive oil, 4 teaspoons of sherry vinegar, and 1 teaspoon of miso paste. Store the dressing in a sealed container in the refrigerator for up to 1 week.

Cioppino

SERVES 4

PREP TIME:
15 minutes

COOK TIME:
30 minutes

Cioppino is a classic fish-based stew dish.

2 tablespoons extra-virgin
  olive oil
Pinch red pepper flakes
1 small yellow onion, diced
2 garlic cloves, thinly sliced
Kosher salt
Freshly ground black pepper
1 (14-ounce) can crushed
  tomatoes, undrained
2 cups low-sodium fish or
  shellfish stock

1 (2-pound) scrubbed
  Dungeness crab, cleaned
  and quartered
16 clams, cleaned
16 mussels, cleaned
12 large (U31/40) shrimp,
  tail-off, peeled, and deveined
1 (4-ounce) salmon fillet, cut
  into 2-inch pieces
4 ounces bay scallops
2 tablespoons minced fresh
  parsley, for garnish
Garlic bread, for serving

1. In a Dutch oven, heat the olive oil and red pepper flakes over
   medium heat. Add the onion and garlic, cover the pot, and cook
   for about 4 minutes, stirring occasionally.

2. Season with salt and pepper and continue to cook, uncovered,
   until the liquid has evaporated, another 2 minutes.

3. Add the tomatoes with their juices and sauté for 3 minutes.
   Add the fish stock, increase the heat to medium-high, and
   bring to a boil. Reduce the heat to medium-low and simmer for
   10 minutes, until the liquid reduces slightly.

4. Add the crab, clams, mussels, shrimp,
   salmon, and scallops. Cover and cook for
   8 to 10 minutes, or until all the seafood
   is cooked.

5. Divide the stew into bowls and garnish
   with the parsley. Serve hot with lots of
   garlic bread.

TIP

*Cioppino can contain
any combination of
fish and seafood.
Calamari, cod, and sea
scallops are all good
substitutes.*

Octopus Stew

SERVES 4

PREP TIME:
45 minutes

COOK TIME:
3 hours

This stew is made for dunking bread. The preparation can be a bit messy and time-intensive, but this special dish is worth the effort.

1 small fresh or frozen and partially thawed octopus
2 tablespoons extra-virgin olive oil
1 medium onion, minced
2 garlic cloves, minced
1 tablespoon minced fresh parsley
1 tablespoon Pimenta Moida (page 218)
½ teaspoon sweet paprika
1 cup red wine
4 ounces tomato sauce
Kosher salt (optional)
8 medium white potatoes, peeled and cut into 1-inch dice

TIP

Pair this dish with bread rolls to sop up the sauce, which is a big part of the experience.

1. Cut the octopus into 1-inch pieces. This process is easiest when the octopus is slightly frozen. If using fresh octopus, pop it in the freezer for about 30 minutes before handling.

2. In a medium stockpot, heat the olive oil over medium heat. Add the onion and cook until golden, about 5 minutes. Add the garlic and parsley and cook for 2 minutes. Add the Pimenta Moida and paprika and stir to combine.

3. Add the red wine, tomato sauce, and octopus. Bring to a boil, then reduce the heat to medium-low, cover, and simmer, stirring occasionally, for 2 hours.

4. Add salt to taste. (Some octopuses are naturally salty; others are not.) Add the potatoes and stir to combine. Simmer until the potatoes are very soft and start to break down and thicken the stew, about 45 minutes.

5. Serve hot. Refrigerate leftovers in an airtight container for up to 3 days.

Mediterranean Cod Stew

SERVES 6

PREP TIME:
10 minutes

COOK TIME:
20 minutes

This robust seafood stew, featuring buttery cod, sweet tomatoes, meaty mushrooms, and fruity olives, is a less labor-intensive variation of traditional fish stews like cioppino and bouillabaisse. Pair it with a fresh salad or a loaf of crusty bread.

2 tablespoons extra-virgin olive oil
1 medium onion, chopped
2 garlic cloves, minced
¾ teaspoon smoked paprika
1 (14.5-ounce) can diced tomatoes, undrained
1 (12-ounce) jar roasted red peppers, drained and chopped

1 cup sliced green or black olives
⅓ cup dry red wine
¼ teaspoon freshly ground black pepper
¼ teaspoon kosher salt or sea salt
1½ pounds cod fillets, cut into 1-inch pieces
3 cups sliced mushrooms (about 8 ounces)

1. In a large stockpot over medium heat, heat the olive oil. Add the onion and cook for 4 minutes, stirring occasionally. Add the garlic and smoked paprika and cook for 1 minute, stirring often.

2. Add the tomatoes with their juices, roasted peppers, olives, wine, pepper, and salt, then turn the heat up to medium-high and bring to a boil. Add the cod and mushrooms, then reduce the heat to medium.

3. Cover and cook for about 10 minutes, stirring a few times, until the cod is cooked through and flakes easily. Serve.

4. Refrigerate leftovers in an airtight container for up to 3 days.

TIP

If you don't have any wine on hand, swap it for 1 tablespoon of red wine vinegar mixed with ½ cup of water.

Creamy Scandinavian Fish Soup

**SERVES
4 TO 6**

PREP TIME:
40 minutes

COOK TIME:
50 minutes

This lighter recipe was created to replicate that creamy quality of classic chowder without changing the flavor profile. The result? A rich, flavorful soup that's velvety in texture without an ounce of dairy.

2 Yukon Gold potatoes, peeled and cut into 1-inch pieces

Kosher salt

3 tablespoons extra-virgin olive oil

1 leek, white part only, thoroughly rinsed and thinly sliced

4 to 6 cups fish stock

1 cup diced carrot

1 cup peeled and diced parsnip or celeriac

¼ cup dry white wine

1 pound cod, cut into 1½-inch pieces

8 ounces shrimp, peeled and deveined

8 ounces clams, cleaned and scrubbed

2 to 3 tablespoons red wine vinegar

1½ teaspoons sugar

Chopped fresh parsley, for garnish

1. In a medium stockpot, combine the potatoes and enough water to cover them. Salt the water. Bring to a boil over high heat and cook for about 20 minutes, or until the potatoes are soft. Reserve ½ cup of the cooking water, drain the potatoes, and set them aside to cool.

2. In a large pot over medium-high heat, heat the oil. Add the leek and sauté for about 3 minutes, until it is light brown. Add the fish stock, carrot, and parsnip. Simmer the soup for 10 to 15 minutes, until the vegetables are tender but not fully cooked.

3. While the vegetables cook, combine the cooked potatoes and reserved cooking liquid in a blender and blend until creamy. Add the potatoes to the soup, along with the white wine.

4. Add the cod. Gently simmer for about 5 minutes, until the fish is cooked through (opaque and flaky). Add the shrimp and clams a couple minutes before the cod is done cooking.

5. Add the vinegar, sugar, and a pinch of salt, adjusting each of these to taste—the soup should have a subtle sweet-and-sour flavor.

6. Garnish with parsley and serve.

7. Refrigerate leftovers in an airtight container for up to 3 days.

New England Clam Chowder

SERVES
4 TO 6

PREP TIME:
15 minutes

COOK TIME:
35 minutes

Also known as Boston chowder or white clam chowder, this version is more popular than its cousin, red or Manhattan clam chowder. In San Francisco, it's served in hollowed-out sourdough bread bowls, but it's no less delicious served in regular bowls with some oyster crackers.

2 large russet potatoes, peeled and cut into ½-inch cubes
Kosher salt
2 tablespoons unsalted butter
3 slices bacon, finely chopped
1 large yellow onion, cut into ¼-inch cubes
2 large celery stalks, cut into ¼-inch cubes

2 garlic cloves, minced
1 bay leaf
3 tablespoons all-purpose flour
4 cups whole milk
4 (6.5-ounce) cans chopped clams
3 or 4 dashes Tabasco sauce
Chopped fresh parsley, for garnish (optional)

1. In a large saucepan, cover the potatoes with cold water and add a generous pinch of salt. Bring to a boil over high heat. Reduce the heat to medium-low, cover, and simmer until the potatoes are tender, about 10 to 12 minutes. Remove from the heat and drain, reserving 2 cups of the cooking water.

2. In a Dutch oven, melt the butter over medium heat. Add the bacon and cook until it begins to brown, about 6 minutes. Add the onion, celery, garlic, and bay leaf. Sauté until the vegetables soften, 5 to 6 minutes.

3. Sprinkle the flour over the vegetables and stir to coat, cooking for 2 minutes (do not allow the flour to brown). Gradually whisk in the milk and add the potatoes, clams with their juices, and Tabasco sauce.

4. Simmer the chowder for 10 minutes, stirring frequently. Taste and add salt if needed. If the chowder becomes too thick, adjust the texture by adding the reserved potato liquid, ¼ cup at a time. Discard the bay leaf and serve in warmed soup bowls garnished with chopped parsley (if using).

TIP

Transform this into corn and shrimp chowder by using 1 cup of fish stock instead of the clam juice and stirring in 1 cup of frozen corn and 1 cup of chopped cooked shrimp.

TIP

When making lobster,
save the shells and freeze
for up to 3 months to
easily whip up a batch
of lobster stock.

Lobster and Corn Chowder

SERVES 6

PREP TIME:
20 minutes

**COOK
TIME:** 1 hour
15 minutes

Lobster and corn lend the perfect amount of sweetness to this rich and savory soup. The depth of flavor is achieved by making a stock separately, enriched with flavors from the corn cobs and lobster. Then, the stock gets combined with all the delicious aromatics, lobster, bacon, and Yukon Gold potatoes. Crusty bread is strongly recommended.

8 tablespoons (1 stick) unsalted butter

6 leeks, thoroughly rinsed, dark green woody ends removed, and chopped, divided

Kosher salt

Freshly ground black pepper

1½ teaspoons tomato paste

⅓ cup cognac

3 large thyme sprigs, bundled with butcher's twine, plus 1 tablespoon chopped leaves

2 bay leaves

4 cups whole milk

2 cups heavy (whipping) cream

¾ cup white wine

3 (1½-pound) cooked lobsters, shells split, meat removed and reserved

3 ears corn, kernels removed and reserved

⅓ pound slab bacon, cut into large dice

3 Yukon Gold potatoes, peeled and cut into 1-inch dice

2 celery stalks, diced

¼ cup minced chives, divided

1. In a large stockpot over medium heat, melt the butter, then add half of the leeks and sauté until translucent, about 3 minutes. Season with salt and pepper.

2. Clear a spot in the center of the pot and add the tomato paste. Toast the paste for a few seconds in the hot spot before sautéing with the leeks. Add the cognac, stirring everything to

Continued on next page ⟶

combine, and simmer for 30 seconds. Add the thyme bundle and bay leaves. Pour in the milk, cream, and wine, stirring everything to combine, before adding the lobster shells and corn cobs. Season with salt and pepper, cover, and simmer on low heat for 40 minutes, stirring occasionally.

3. In a Dutch oven (or another large pot) over medium heat, cook the bacon until it is nicely browned and crispy, about 8 minutes. Remove the cooked bacon with a slotted spoon to a paper towel–lined plate and set it aside. Add the potatoes, celery, remaining leeks, corn kernels, and remaining 1 tablespoon of thyme. Season with salt and pepper. Sauté for 5 minutes, or until the potatoes have taken on a little color and the leeks are translucent.

4. Remove the corn cobs and lobster shells from the stockpot. Using a large strainer, strain the remaining stock into the pot with the potatoes, leeks, and corn. Taste and season with salt and pepper. Simmer until the potatoes are fork-tender, about 20 minutes. Add the cooked lobster meat and half of the chives. Simmer until the lobster is warmed through.

5. Remove the thyme sprigs and bay leaves and spoon the chowder into serving bowls. Top with the remaining chives and the bacon. Serve with lots of crusty bread and white wine, if desired.

Spicy Thai Coconut Shrimp Soup

SERVES 4

PREP TIME:
15 minutes

COOK TIME:
25 minutes

The key to this recipe is to be mindful of how much red curry paste you use. It's a spicy base in Thai cooking, and a little can go a long way. If you find it too hot, balance it out with more sugar and lime juice.

2 tablespoons coconut oil

2 lemongrass stalks, peeled down to the core, smashed flat, and minced

3 garlic cloves, minced

1 (1-inch) piece fresh ginger, peeled and minced

1 large red bell pepper, seeded and cut into ½-inch cubes

Pinch kosher salt, plus more as needed

2 tablespoons red curry paste

1 (13.5-ounce) can full-fat coconut milk

Zest and juice of 1 lime

1 tablespoon packed light brown sugar

1 cup water

1 pound medium shrimp (U41/50), tail-off, peeled, and deveined

1 tablespoon fish sauce (optional)

2 tablespoons roughly chopped cilantro, divided

2 cups cooked white rice

1 lime, cut into 4 wedges, for serving

Sliced scallions, for garnish

1. Melt the coconut oil in a medium saucepan or Dutch oven over medium-high heat. Sauté the lemongrass, garlic, and ginger until fragrant, 2 to 3 minutes.

2. Add the bell pepper and cook for 3 minutes more, or until soft. Add the salt. You may need to turn the heat down to keep the aromatics from burning. Add the curry paste and stir quickly to sauté and combine with the vegetables, about 1 minute.

3. Add the coconut milk, lime zest, lime juice, brown sugar, and water. Reduce the heat to medium-low and simmer, stirring occasionally, for about 5 minutes.

Continued on next page ⟶

4. Season the shrimp with the fish sauce (if using) or a pinch of salt and add the shrimp to the soup. Simmer for 10 to 12 minutes, or until the shrimp are pink and opaque. Turn off the heat and stir in 1 tablespoon of cilantro.

5. To serve, evenly divide the cooked rice among four warmed soup bowls. Divide the soup and shrimp among the bowls and top with the remaining 1 tablespoon of cilantro. Serve with the lime wedges and garnish with sliced scallions.

TIP

Crabmeat makes an excellent substitution here. You can also switch the red curry paste for a milder, sweeter yellow curry paste.

TIP

Bay scallops are often smaller than sea scallops and can be found frozen. Be sure to thaw frozen scallops before adding them to the pan. Add the seafood last so it doesn't overcook and become rubbery.

Seafood Gumbo-laya

SERVES 6

PREP TIME:
10 minutes

COOK TIME:
30 minutes

There are differences between Cajun and Creole cuisine, but this gumbo and jambalaya hybrid is sure to become a favorite one-skillet meal. The deep flavor usually comes from a roux, but this recipe lets you skip that step to get dinner on the table more quickly.

2 tablespoons canola oil

3 celery stalks, diced

1 yellow onion, diced

1 green bell pepper, seeded and diced

3 garlic cloves, minced

2 bay leaves

1 teaspoon Creole seasoning

1/4 teaspoon ground cayenne pepper

1/8 teaspoon freshly ground black pepper

1/2 (6-ounce) can no-salt-added tomato paste

1 cup sliced frozen okra

1 (28-ounce) can crushed tomatoes, undrained

2 cups vegetable or seafood stock

1 pound shrimp, tail-off, peeled, and deveined

1/2 pound bay scallops

6 cups cooked rice

Fresh parsley, for garnish (optional)

1. Heat the oil in a large saucepan or Dutch oven over medium-high heat. Add the celery, onion, bell pepper, and garlic. Cook for 2 to 3 minutes, until it becomes fragrant, then add the bay leaves, Creole seasoning, cayenne pepper, and black pepper. Stir to combine, then add the tomato paste and cook for 2 to 3 minutes more.

2. Add the okra, tomatoes with their juices, and stock. Stir to combine and simmer, covered, stirring occasionally, for 20 minutes.

3. Add the shrimp and scallops. Simmer for another 3 to 4 minutes, or until the seafood is fully cooked. The shrimp and scallops should be opaque. Serve over the cooked rice and garnish with fresh parsley (if using).

Lemony Cod, Potato, and Leek Chowder

SERVES 4

PREP TIME:
10 minutes

COOK TIME:
45 minutes

This cozy soup is caught somewhere between a potato-leek soup and a clam chowder, and the results are deliciously laced with notes of white wine, thyme, and bacon. Cod works well in this soup because of its mildness and ability to maintain structural integrity while simmering.

4 ounces bacon, cut into
⅓-inch chunks

2 tablespoons unsalted butter

1 tablespoon extra-virgin
olive oil

3 celery stalks, chopped

2 leeks, thoroughly rinsed,
dark green woody ends
removed, halved lengthwise,
and cut into ¼-inch-thick
half-moons

Kosher salt

Freshly ground black pepper

2 large Yukon Gold potatoes,
peeled and cut into
½-inch dice

5 garlic cloves, roughly
chopped

2 tablespoons chopped fresh
parsley

½ teaspoon red pepper flakes

4 thyme sprigs

1 cup white wine

2½ cups seafood stock

1 teaspoon lemon zest

1½ pounds cod fillets, skinned
and cut into 2-by-3-inch
pieces

2 cups heavy (whipping)
cream

¼ cup minced chives, for
serving

Lemon wedges, for serving

1. Cook the bacon in a Dutch oven over medium heat until browned but not crisp, 6 to 7 minutes. Transfer it to a paper towel–lined plate.

2. Melt the butter and olive oil in the Dutch oven over medium-high heat. Add the celery, leeks, and a pinch of salt and black pepper. Sauté until translucent, 2 to 3 minutes. Add

the potatoes, garlic, parsley, red pepper flakes, and thyme and sauté until fragrant, 20 to 30 seconds.

3. Add the wine and deglaze, scraping any browned bits off the bottom of the pan. Simmer for 2 minutes more. Pour in the seafood stock. Bring to a boil, then reduce the heat to low and simmer until the potatoes are fork-tender, about 15 minutes. Stir in the lemon zest.

4. Season the cod with salt and pepper. Add to the soup. Cover and simmer until the fish is opaque and you can see the definition of where it would flake, about 7 minutes, depending on the thickness of the fillets.

5. Pour in the cream and simmer for 10 minutes more. The fish will break into smaller pieces at this point. Discard the thyme sprigs. Serve with the bacon pieces, minced chives, and lemon wedges.

Tortilla Soup with Grilled Shrimp

SERVES 4

PREP TIME:
20 minutes

COOK TIME:
55 minutes

Grilled shrimp take this soup to the next level, while the tortillas blended into the tomatoes, smoky poblano peppers, and aromatics contribute to its delicious flavor and creamy texture.

1 poblano pepper

5 tomatoes, quartered

1 yellow onion, cut into 1-inch chunks

4 garlic cloves, peeled and smashed

4 tablespoons extra-virgin olive oil, divided, plus more for drizzling

Kosher salt

Freshly ground black pepper

½ teaspoon chili powder

¼ teaspoon ground cumin

4½ cups chicken stock

2 tablespoons red wine vinegar

10 (6-inch) corn tortillas, cut into ½-inch-thick strips, divided

12 ounces shrimp, tail-on, peeled, and deveined

1 avocado, peeled, pitted, and diced

1 cup chopped fresh cilantro

Sour cream, for serving

Cotija cheese, crumbled, for serving

Lime wedges, for serving

1. Preheat the oven to 400°F. Line a baking sheet with parchment paper.

2. Carefully place the poblano over an open gas flame on medium heat. Rotate regularly, charring and blistering. Alternatively, char the poblano under the broiler. Watch it closely to make sure it doesn't burn, turning every couple of minutes until charred. Transfer to a heatproof bowl, cover with plastic wrap and let steam for 5 minutes. Remove the skin, stem, and seeds. Cut the pepper into quarters and set aside.

3. Combine the tomatoes, poblano, onion, and garlic on the baking sheet. Drizzle with 3 tablespoons of olive oil. Season with salt, pepper, chili powder, and cumin and stir to mix. Roast for 15 minutes, until the onions are translucent and the tomatoes begin to release their juices.

4. Heat the remaining 1 tablespoon of olive oil in a large Dutch oven over medium-high heat. Add the poblano mixture and sizzle for 1 to 2 minutes. Add the stock, vinegar, and half of the tortillas. Season with salt and pepper. Bring to a boil, then reduce the heat to low and simmer for 30 minutes.

5. On a parchment paper–lined baking sheet, toss the remaining tortilla strips with a drizzle of olive oil and sprinkle of salt. Bake until golden brown, 5 to 7 minutes, tossing halfway through.

6. Prepare a grill and bring the temperature to medium-high heat (400°F to 450°F). Season the shrimp with olive oil, salt, and pepper. Grill 1 to 2 minutes per side, until pink.

7. Using an immersion blender (or working in batches with a blender), puree the soup until smooth. Season with salt and pepper to taste.

8. Serve with the shrimp, baked tortilla strips, avocado, cilantro, sour cream, cotija, and lime wedges.

Halibut and White Bean Minestrone

SERVES 4

PREP TIME:
15 minutes

COOK TIME:
55 minutes

Warming minestrone gets a seafood twist. This soup is best served with lots of rustic, crusty bread.

3 celery stalks, diced
1 yellow onion, diced
1 carrot, diced
4 garlic cloves, chopped
4 thyme sprigs
2 rosemary sprigs
2 tablespoons extra-virgin
  olive oil
6 ounces pancetta, cut into
  small dice
2 tablespoons tomato paste
½ cup dry white wine
½ cup roughly chopped fresh
  Italian parsley

1 (15-ounce) can white beans,
  drained and rinsed
3½ cups seafood stock
1 (28-ounce) can tomato
  passata or tomato puree
  (preferably San Marzano)
Kosher salt
Freshly ground black pepper
2 pounds halibut fillets
Parmigiano-Reggiano cheese,
  for serving
Crusty bread, for serving

1. Use a food processor to finely chop the celery, onion, carrot, and garlic.

2. Bundle the thyme and rosemary together with kitchen twine.

3. Heat the olive oil in a Dutch oven over medium heat. Add the pancetta and sauté until it is lightly brown but not crispy, about 2 minutes. Add the vegetable mixture and tomato paste, sautéing to combine, about 2 minutes.

4. Pour in the wine, then add the thyme and rosemary sprigs, parsley, and white beans, stirring to combine. Simmer for 1 to 2 minutes more. Stir in the seafood stock and tomato passata and season with salt and pepper.

5. Bring to a boil, then reduce the heat to low and simmer for 30 minutes.

6. Season the halibut fillets with salt and pepper and gently place them in the soup. Simmer for about 15 minutes, until the fish is opaque and gently flakes apart into large pieces.

7. Season with salt and pepper to taste. Spoon the soup into bowls and top with Parmigiano-Reggiano cheese. Serve with crusty bread.

TIP

Instead of halibut fillets, you can also use flounder, cod, sole, or tilapia in this minestrone. Use the same amount of one or try a mix of two types.

Lobster Bisque

SERVES 4

PREP TIME:
15 minutes

COOK TIME:
50 minutes

This easy version of lobster bisque makes whipping it up at home an absolute breeze. Since we forego homemade lobster stock, we build depth of flavor by combining a mirepoix—a mixture of carrots, celery, and onion—with rich tomato paste, plenty of fresh herbs, dry white wine, and sherry.

3 tablespoons unsalted butter
1 tablespoon extra-virgin olive oil
1 large yellow onion, minced
2 celery stalks, minced
2 carrots, peeled and minced
2½ tablespoons tomato paste (preferably triple concentrated)
4 garlic cloves, roughly chopped
Kosher salt
Freshly ground black pepper

2 tablespoons all-purpose flour
1 cup dry white wine
½ cup sherry
2 bay leaves
4 thyme sprigs
4½ cups seafood stock
¾ cup heavy (whipping) cream
1¼ pounds cooked lobster meat, chopped
4 tablespoons minced chives, for serving

1. Heat the butter and oil in a large Dutch oven over medium-high heat. Add the onion, celery, and carrots and sauté until the onions are translucent and the carrots are beginning to soften, about 3 minutes.

2. In the center of the pan, add the tomato paste and garlic and sauté until fragrant, about 45 seconds. Season with salt and pepper. Sprinkle the flour over the mixture, sautéing to cook the raw taste out of the flour and impart some of the flavors from the pan.

3. Pour in the wine a little at a time, then the sherry, thoroughly scraping the bottom of the pan with a wooden spoon. Add the bay leaves and thyme sprigs and simmer until the liquid is reduced slightly, about 1 minute.

4. Add the stock and bring it to a boil. Reduce the heat to low and simmer for 35 minutes.

5. Remove the soup from the heat and discard the thyme sprigs and bay leaves. Using an immersion blender (or working in batches with a blender), blend the soup until smooth.

6. Return to a low simmer and stir in the heavy cream and lobster meat. Simmer for 5 to 7 minutes.

7. Divide the soup evenly among four bowls and top each with 1 tablespoon of chives.

TIP

Shrimp is a fantastic swap in this lobster bisque. Simply replace the lobster meat with the same amount of peeled, deveined, and chopped shrimp.

Provençal Fish Stew

SERVES 6

PREP TIME:
1 hour

COOK TIME:
50 minutes

The Provençal region of France—particularly Marseille—is known for its seafood stews. One famous dish is bouillabaisse, which features many types of fish and shellfish with notes of saffron and fennel and takes two days to complete. Although this stew was inspired by the Marseille classic, it is much less time-consuming and features a pared-down selection of whitefish, clams, and mussels.

10 littleneck clams, scrubbed
10 mussels
3 tablespoons extra-virgin olive oil
1 onion, chopped
2 celery stalks, diced
1 carrot, peeled and diced
2 small Yukon Gold potatoes, peeled and cut into ½-inch dice
½ large fennel bulb, chopped, fronds reserved for garnish
Kosher salt

Freshly ground black pepper
6 garlic cloves, roughly chopped
1 teaspoon lemon zest
2½ cups chopped Roma tomatoes, with their juices
¾ cup white wine
3 cups seafood stock
1½ pounds whitefish fillets, such as halibut, haddock, cod, or other firm whitefish
½ cup chopped fresh parsley, for serving

1. Place the clams in a bowl of salted water for 30 minutes to purge them of any sand. Pick the clams out individually. Discard the water and rinse the bowl thoroughly before returning the clams to the bowl and soaking for 15 minutes more. Pick the clams out of the water individually when done.

2. Place the mussels in a colander and run under cold water, using your hands to rid them of dirt and debris. If any mussels appear to be slightly open, tap them. If they close in response, they are alive and safe to eat. If they do not close, discard them.

Debeard the mussels by pinching the hairlike fibers with your thumb and forefinger and tugging them toward the hinge of the shell.

3. Heat the oil over medium-high heat in a Dutch oven. Add the onion, celery, and carrot, sautéing until the onion is translucent, about 2 minutes. Stir in the potatoes and fennel and season with salt and pepper. Sauté until the fennel is translucent, another 2 minutes. Add the garlic and lemon zest and sauté until the garlic is fragrant, about 30 seconds. Add the tomatoes and white wine. Using a wooden spoon, scrape the bottom of the pot. Cook for 1½ minutes.

4. Pour in the stock and season with salt and pepper. Bring the soup to a boil, then reduce the heat to low and simmer for 30 minutes. Season with salt and pepper to taste.

5. Add the whitefish and cook for 5 minutes. Add the clams and mussels and cook for 8 minutes more. Discard any clams or mussels that do not open.

6. Spoon into bowls and serve topped with parsley.

Fregola and Clams in Tomato-Marsala Broth

SERVES 4

PREP TIME:
55 minutes

COOK TIME:
30 minutes

Fregola makes a toothsome addition to briny clams nestled in an aromatic tomato-marsala broth. Do not skimp on the baguettes—you'll want to sop up all the sauce you can.

24 littleneck clams, scrubbed
3 cups chicken stock
3 cups water
8 ounces fregola
3 tablespoons unsalted butter
2 tablespoons extra-virgin olive oil, plus more for drizzling
1 shallot, minced
Kosher salt
1½ cups cherry tomatoes, halved

7 garlic cloves, chopped
3 thyme sprigs, stems removed, chopped
1 tablespoon tomato paste
½ teaspoon red pepper flakes
1 cup dry marsala wine
2 cups seafood stock
1 baguette, sliced into ½-inch-thick pieces
½ cup chopped fresh Italian parsley

1. Place the clams in a bowl of salted water for 30 minutes to purge them of sand. Pick the clams out individually. Discard the water and thoroughly rinse the bowl before returning the clams to the bowl and soaking for 15 minutes more. Pick the clams out of the water individually when done.

2. Preheat the oven to 425°F.

3. In a large stockpot, bring the chicken stock and water to a boil. Add the fregola and cook until al dente, about 8 to 9 minutes. Reserve 1 cup of cooking liquid before draining. Set aside.

4. Heat the butter and olive oil in a large Dutch oven over medium heat. Add the shallot, season with salt, and sauté until translucent, about 1 minute. Add the tomatoes, garlic, thyme, tomato paste, and red pepper flakes and sauté for 1 minute.

5. Pour in the marsala, then add the clams, tossing to coat. Pour in the stock, season with salt, cover, and steam for 7 to 8 minutes. Discard any clams that do not open. Taste for seasoning and adjust.

6. While the clams are cooking, place the baguette slices on a large baking sheet. Drizzle with olive oil, season with salt, and bake for 6 to 10 minutes, until golden brown.

7. Spoon the fregola over the clams. Ladle the soup into bowls, top with the parsley, and serve alongside the baguette slices.

TIP

Feel free to replace the clams with mussels or the fregola with Israeli couscous.

Rustic Italian Seafood Stew

SERVES 4

PREP TIME:
20 minutes

COOK TIME:
50 minutes

This rustic seafood stew has notes of cioppino inspiration; however, it is slightly simpler, featuring whitefish fillets, scallops, and shrimp that cook in a flash.

3 tablespoons extra-virgin olive oil

1 celery stalk, diced

1 large yellow onion, diced

Kosher salt

6 garlic cloves, roughly chopped

1 teaspoon chopped fresh thyme

1 teaspoon chopped fresh oregano

Pinch red pepper flakes

1 cup tomato passata or tomato puree (preferably San Marzano)

Freshly ground black pepper

1 cup dry white wine

1¼ cups seafood stock

8 ounces whitefish fillets, such as cod or haddock, cut into roughly 3-inch pieces

8 ounces shrimp, peeled and deveined, cut into large bite-size pieces

8 ounces scallops, muscle removed, cut into large bite-size pieces

¼ cup chopped fresh Italian parsley

Rustic crusty bread, for serving

1. Heat the olive oil in a large Dutch oven over medium heat. Add the celery and onion, season with salt, and cook until the onion is translucent, about 1 minute. Add the garlic, thyme, oregano, and red pepper flakes and sauté until the garlic is fragrant, 20 to 30 seconds.

2. Pour in the tomato passata and season with salt and pepper, being sure to scrape up the bottom of the pan with a wooden spoon. Once the sauce is simmering, pour in the wine. Simmer for 30 seconds, then pour in the stock.

3. Bring to a boil, then reduce the heat to low and simmer for 35 to 40 minutes to allow the flavors to develop. Taste for seasoning before adding the seafood.

4. Add the fish fillets and cook for 5 to 7 minutes. Check to see the fish is opaque throughout before adding the shrimp and scallops and cooking for another 2 minutes.

5. Add the parsley and season to taste. Ladle the soup into bowls and serve with lots of crusty bread.

Creamy Roasted Tomato and Halibut Chowder

SERVES 6

PREP TIME:
15 minutes

**COOK
TIME:** 1 hour
5 minutes

This creamy roasted tomato and halibut chowder features Manhattan-style chowder flavors but seems to have married a creamy tomato soup and is more delicious for it. Serve this soup alongside charred, crusty bread (or even a good grilled cheese), a crisp green salad, and something cold and bubbly.

2½ pounds Roma tomatoes
8 garlic cloves, peeled and
 smashed
1 large yellow onion, cut into
 large chunks
Extra-virgin olive oil, for
 drizzling
Kosher salt
Freshly ground black pepper
5 tablespoons unsalted butter
¾ cup white wine

2 tablespoons chopped fresh
 thyme
4½ cups seafood stock or
 chicken stock
2 bay leaves
¾ cup heavy (whipping)
 cream
1 pound halibut fillets,
 skinned and cut into 2-inch
 pieces

1. Preheat the oven to 450°F. Spread the tomatoes, garlic, and onion out on a baking sheet. Drizzle generously with olive oil and season with salt and pepper. Roast for 30 minutes, tossing halfway through.

2. In a large Dutch oven over medium heat, melt the butter. Add the tomato mixture from the baking sheet, allowing everything to come to a sizzle. Add the wine and thyme and simmer for 30 to 45 seconds, scraping the bottom of the pot with a wooden spoon. Pour in the stock, add the bay leaves, and bring to a boil. Reduce the heat to low and simmer for 25 minutes.

3. Remove the bay leaves. Using an immersion blender (or working in batches with a blender), blend the soup until smooth. Add the cream, taste for seasoning, and adjust with salt and pepper. Season the halibut fillets with salt and pepper and add to the soup. Cover and simmer 5 to 7 minutes, until the fish is cooked through. Serve.

4. Refrigerate leftovers in a sealed container for up to 3 days.

TIP

Feel free to use skinless snapper or cod fillets in this soup instead of the halibut.

5

EASY WEEKNIGHT DINNERS

Sheet Pan Salmon with Potatoes and Asparagus

SERVES 4

PREP TIME:
15 minutes

COOK TIME:
20 minutes

ONE POT

5-INGREDIENT

This recipe is the perfect weeknight dinner for when you're craving something light and nutritious. An assortment of healthy ingredients, tossed together on a baking sheet and roasted in the oven, are the perfect blank canvas to customize with whatever aromatics you have on hand.

2 tablespoons extra-virgin olive oil, plus more for brushing

4 (6-ounce) wild Alaskan salmon fillets

1 pound red potatoes, cut into 1-inch pieces

1 bunch asparagus, woody ends removed

1 teaspoon herbes de Provence

Kosher salt

1 cup cherry tomatoes or grape tomatoes, halved crosswise

1. Preheat the oven to 400°F. Brush a large baking sheet with olive oil.

2. Place the salmon on one side of the baking sheet and brush it with olive oil.

3. Place the potatoes and asparagus on the other side of the baking sheet, toss with the olive oil and herbes de Provence, and sprinkle with salt.

4. Bake for about 20 minutes, turning the vegetables halfway through, until the salmon is cooked throughout (145°F) and the potatoes and asparagus are tender and golden. Remove any components early, if needed, to avoid overcooking; the potatoes, for example, may take longer than the other items.

5. Transfer the potatoes and asparagus to a platter and scatter the tomatoes over the top. Top with the salmon and serve.

Honey and Creole Mustard–Glazed Salmon with Pecans

SERVES 6

PREP TIME:
10 minutes

COOK TIME:
10 minutes

30 MINUTES
OR LESS

These salmon fillets are glazed with honey and Creole mustard, topped with chopped pecans, and broiled. Wild-caught salmon are preferred because the farmed variety are given color enhancers to make their skin unnaturally pink, but feel free to use the farmed kind in this recipe; it will taste just as good.

2 tablespoons honey
2 tablespoons Creole mustard
6 (6-ounce) salmon fillets, skin-on

1 tablespoon unsalted butter, melted
½ teaspoon Cajun Spice Blend (page 217)
¼ cup chopped pecans

1. Preheat the oven to broil.

2. In a small bowl, combine the honey and mustard until well mixed.

3. Place the fillets, skin-side down, on a baking sheet or broiler pan and lightly brush with the melted butter.

4. Evenly brush the mustard mixture on the fillets, then season with the Cajun Spice Blend.

5. Sprinkle the pecans evenly over the fillets. Place the pan 6 to 8 inches from the broiler and cook for 8 to 10 minutes, or until the fish flakes easily with fork. Serve immediately.

TIP

You can change up this recipe by using a different fish. Any firm-fleshed fish will work, including red snapper, redfish, tuna, swordfish, or Spanish mackerel.

a

Slow-Roasted Dijon Arctic Char

SERVES 4

PREP TIME:
10 minutes

COOK TIME:
20 minutes

30 MINUTES
OR LESS

ONE POT

5-INGREDIENT

Keep this recipe in your back pocket for when you're in a rush to make dinner and don't know what to do with a piece of fish. Although the recipe says "slow-roasted," the fish cooks so quickly that you can prepare this recipe in 30 minutes. Turning down the oven temperature and layering Dijon mustard on top of a beautiful fillet ensures the fish doesn't dry out.

4 (6-ounce) arctic char fillets
1 teaspoon smoked paprika
¼ teaspoon salt
¼ teaspoon freshly ground
  black pepper

¼ cup Dijon mustard
1 teaspoon light or dark
  brown sugar

TIP

Arctic char not available or in season? Use salmon instead.

1. Preheat the oven to 300°F.
2. Place the arctic char fillets on a baking sheet. Season with the smoked paprika, salt, and pepper. Spread the mustard on top of the fish and sprinkle the brown sugar on top.
3. Roast the fish for 20 minutes, until it flakes easily with a fork.

TIP

Trout with skin is often found as an intact whole fish. If you prefer not to debone the fillets, ask your fishmonger to do this for you. If you purchase trout as individual fillets with the skin removed, be careful when searing so they don't break apart in the skillet.

Pan-Seared Trout with Edamame Succotash

SERVES 4

PREP TIME:
10 minutes

COOK TIME:
15 minutes

30 MINUTES
OR LESS

Traditional succotash is made with lima beans, but this recipe calls for edamame, which brings more texture to this dish. To thaw frozen shelled edamame in advance, defrost in the refrigerator overnight or submerge in water before cooking.

1 tablespoon unsalted butter
1½ cups sweet corn kernels
1½ cups frozen shelled edamame, thawed
1 zucchini, diced
1 cup halved cherry tomatoes
Pinch salt, plus more for seasoning

Pinch freshly ground black pepper, plus more for seasoning
6 to 8 fresh basil leaves, chopped
1 tablespoon canola oil
4 trout fillets, skin-on
2 lemons, cut into wedges

1. Melt the butter in a large skillet over medium-high heat. Add the corn, edamame, and zucchini, cook for 3 to 5 minutes, then stir in the tomatoes, salt, and pepper. Remove the mixture from the skillet and transfer to a serving bowl. Season with salt and pepper and sprinkle the basil on top.

2. Return the skillet to medium-high heat and add the canola oil. Once the oil is heated, add the trout, skin-side down. Sear for about 6 minutes, then carefully flip the fillets and cook for another 1 to 2 minutes.

3. To serve, plate each trout fillet over a quarter of the vegetable mixture and squeeze the lemon wedges over the top.

Spicy Tuna Poke

SERVES 4

PREP TIME:
15 minutes

30 MINUTES
OR LESS

A chopped salad of raw tuna for dinner is the perfect meal on a hot summer night. Poke is now very popular here on the mainland, even though it's been a staple in Hawaii for generations, and for good reason: It's simple to make and delicious as an appetizer or a light meal. Make sure to select the finest quality ahi tuna your budget allows.

1½ tablespoons soy sauce

2 teaspoons sesame oil

1 teaspoon honey

1 teaspoon sriracha

12 ounces raw sushi-grade ahi tuna, cut into ½-inch cubes

3 scallions, white and green parts, thinly sliced

Kosher salt

Freshly ground black pepper

1 tablespoon furikake

1. In a medium bowl, whisk together the soy sauce, sesame oil, honey, and sriracha.

2. Fold in the tuna and scallions, then season with salt and pepper to taste. Transfer to a chilled serving bowl and sprinkle the furikake over the top. Serve immediately.

TIP

To make bowls with this recipe, add the poke to a bowl of cooked white rice, sliced vegetables, diced avocado, edamame, and a few lime wedges for a hit of brightness. Also, there is no such thing as too much furikake.

Red Snapper Veracruz

SERVES 4

PREP TIME:
15 minutes

COOK TIME:
40 minutes

This classic Mexican dish tastes even better the next day. The snapper gets simmered directly in the sauce instead of pan-frying the fish separately for a simpler take.

4 (6- to 8-ounce) red snapper fillets
Kosher salt
Freshly ground black pepper
Juice of 2 limes, divided
2 tablespoons extra-virgin olive oil
1 medium yellow onion, cut into long, thin strips
1 large red bell pepper, seeded and cut into ¼-inch-wide strips
3 garlic cloves, minced

1 teaspoon chili powder
1 teaspoon dried oregano
1 (14-ounce) can diced tomatoes, undrained
½ cup pitted green olives, roughly chopped
1 tablespoon capers, roughly chopped

TIP

Serve this over Spanish rice or with warm tortillas. Garnish with chopped cilantro. You can also use tilapia, halibut, or cod in this dish if snapper is not available.

1. Pat the fish dry and season with salt and pepper. Squeeze half of the lime juice over the top and set aside.

2. Heat the olive oil in a wide, shallow sauté pan over medium-high heat. When the oil starts to smoke, sauté the onion and bell pepper until the onion is soft and translucent, about 7 minutes. Season lightly with salt and pepper. Add the garlic, chili powder, and oregano and continue sautéing for 1 minute more. Reduce the heat to medium and add the tomatoes and their juices, olives, and capers and simmer for 8 to 10 minutes.

3. Add the fish to the sauce and cover. Simmer for 15 to 20 minutes, or until the fish flakes when pushed with a fork. Squeeze the remaining lime juice over the top and serve hot.

Sardine Breakfast

SERVES 4

PREP TIME:
10 minutes

COOK TIME:
25 minutes

A fisherman's breakfast is like corned beef hash, except it is served with sardines instead. Pair with lightly charred baguette slices for the ultimate bite.

2 (4.5-ounce) cans oil-packed sardines, oil drained and reserved

2 Roma tomatoes, cut into ¼-inch dice

1 small red onion, cut into ¼-inch dice

1 small pasilla pepper, cut into ¼-inch dice

3 garlic cloves, minced

1 tablespoon capers, rinsed and chopped

Kosher salt

Freshly ground black pepper

2 large eggs

1 tablespoon chopped fresh dill, for garnish

1. Preheat the oven to 400°F. Place a 10-inch cast-iron skillet in the oven.

2. In a medium bowl, break the sardines into chunks. Mix in the tomatoes, onion, pasilla pepper, garlic, and capers until thoroughly combined. Season with salt and pepper and add 2 tablespoons of the reserved sardine oil.

3. Transfer the mixture to the preheated skillet and bake for 15 minutes.

4. Remove the skillet from the oven. Using the back of a large kitchen spoon, make two shallow depressions in the mixture. Crack an egg into each depression and season with salt and pepper. Bake for 8 minutes, or until the eggs have just set.

5. Remove the skillet from the oven, tent with aluminum foil, and allow to rest for 2 to 3 minutes. Garnish with the chopped dill and serve immediately.

> **TIP**
>
> *If you would like to use fresh sardines, cut them into bite-size chunks and mix them raw with the vegetables. Increase the cooking time by 5 minutes before adding the eggs.*

Cod in Tomato Sauce

**SERVES
2 TO 4**

Serve this light and bright dish on top of quinoa or rice or with crusty bread to soak up all that sauce.

PREP TIME:
5 minutes

COOK TIME:
30 minutes

**30 MINUTES
OR LESS**

2 tablespoons extra-virgin olive oil, plus more for drizzling
1 yellow onion, halved, then cut into 1/4-inch-thick slices
Kosher salt
Freshly ground black pepper
6 garlic cloves, chopped
3 tablespoons chopped fresh thyme, divided

1 tablespoon chopped fresh rosemary
1/4 teaspoon red pepper flakes
4 cups diced Roma tomatoes
3/4 cup dry white wine
2 cups panko bread crumbs
1 pound cod, cut into 4 portions
1 lemon, cut into wedges, for serving

1. Preheat the oven to 425°F.

2. Heat the olive oil in a cast-iron skillet over medium heat. Once hot, add the onion and season with salt and pepper. Sauté until translucent, about 3 minutes, then add the garlic, 2 tablespoons of thyme, the rosemary, and red pepper flakes. Sauté until fragrant, about 30 seconds. Add the tomatoes and a pinch of salt. Stir to combine and simmer for 2 minutes.

3. Add the wine and deglaze the pan by scraping the bottom with a wooden spoon. Increase the heat to medium-high and simmer for 30 seconds. Gently crush the tomatoes with the back of a wooden spoon to help release their juices.

4. In a small bowl, mix the bread crumbs and the remaining 1 tablespoon of thyme. Season with salt and pepper and drizzle with olive oil so the mixture resembles slightly damp sand.

5. Season the cod with salt and pepper. Nestle the cod into the sauce and sprinkle with the panko. Bake until the fish is opaque, 15 to 20 minutes. Serve with the lemon wedges.

TIP

Feel free to use halibut if you can't find cod.

Sardines with White Beans and Peppers

SERVES 4

PREP TIME:
10 minutes

COOK TIME:
10 minutes

30 MINUTES
OR LESS

ONE POT

This bright and fresh seafood salad was inspired by a recipe from a PBS cooking show with Jacques Pépin.

3 tablespoons extra-virgin olive oil or oil drained from the sardine can, divided
1 large red bell pepper, seeded and cut into ¼-inch-thick strips
Kosher salt
Freshly ground black pepper
3 garlic cloves, minced

1 (15-ounce) can cannellini beans, drained and rinsed
2 teaspoons smoked paprika
1 (4.5-ounce) can oil-packed sardines
1 tablespoon sherry vinegar or red wine vinegar
2 large handfuls baby kale or wild arugula

1. Heat a large nonstick skillet over medium heat. Add 2 tablespoons of olive oil and swirl to coat the pan. When the oil is warm, add the bell pepper and sauté for 4 minutes, or until it begins to soften. Season with salt and pepper.

2. Add the garlic and sauté for a few more seconds. Add the beans and paprika and sauté for 2 minutes, or until the beans start to brown slightly.

3. Add the sardines and toss gently to combine, breaking up the sardines into smaller chunks. Keep folding gently until the sardines are warmed through.

4. Remove the pan from the heat and allow it to cool slightly. Add the vinegar and kale, seasoning with a pinch of salt and pepper. The heat should wilt the kale slightly. Drizzle the remaining 1 tablespoon of olive oil over the salad and serve warm.

TIP

Canned smoked mackerel is excellent in this salad as well. Instead of using kale or arugula, toss in handfuls of frisée or baby lettuce.

Pantry Bucatini with Anchovies and Bread Crumbs

SERVES 4

PREP TIME:
5 minutes

COOK TIME:
15 minutes

30 MINUTES
OR LESS

You'll see this recipe calls for an entire tube of tomato paste; please use the triple-concentrated stuff. It's available at most grocery stores, and its depth of flavor is unmatched by the less-concentrated varieties.

4 tablespoons extra-virgin olive oil, divided
1 cup panko bread crumbs
1 tablespoon chopped fresh thyme
Kosher salt
Freshly ground black pepper
1 pound bucatini
2 shallots, thinly sliced

6 anchovies, chopped
¼ teaspoon red pepper flakes
3 garlic cloves, minced
1 (4.5-ounce) tube triple-concentrated tomato paste
Parmigiano-Reggiano cheese, freshly grated, for serving

1. Bring a large pot of salted water to a rolling boil over high heat.
2. Heat 1 tablespoon of olive oil in a small skillet over medium-low heat. Add the bread crumbs, thyme, and a pinch of salt and pepper. Cook, stirring constantly, until golden brown, about 2 minutes. Transfer to a plate and set aside.
3. Add the bucatini to the pot of boiling water and cook until al dente, about 8 minutes. Reserve ¾ cup of the cooking water before draining the bucatini.
4. While the bucatini is cooking, heat the remaining 3 tablespoons of oil in a large skillet over medium heat. Add the shallots and a pinch of salt. Sauté for 1 minute. Stir in the anchovies and red pepper flakes. Next, add the garlic and sauté until fragrant, about 30 seconds. Add the entire tube of tomato paste, stirring well to cook out the raw flavor.

Continued on next page ⟶

5. Transfer the bucatini directly to the tomato-anchovy-shallot mixture along with ¼ cup of pasta water. Toss to thoroughly combine, adding more pasta water as needed to create a silky sauce. Add a handful of Parmigiano-Reggiano cheese and thoroughly toss to combine. Top with the bread crumbs and more grated cheese.

6. Refrigerate in a sealed container for 2 to 3 days.

Smoked Mackerel Kedgeree

SERVES 4

PREP TIME:
25 minutes

COOK TIME:
15 minutes

30 MINUTES
OR LESS

Kedgeree originates from India's kitchari, a lightly spiced rice and lentil dish. Smoked fish is flaked into the rice to make it a breakfast dish. It's a celebration of assertive flavors and the blending of cultures.

1 cup basmati rice
2 large eggs
3 tablespoons unsalted
  butter
1 shallot, cut into ¼-inch
  cubes
Kosher salt
1 tablespoon curry powder
1 cup low-sodium chicken
  stock

2 (4-ounce) cans oil-packed
  smoked mackerel, drained
  and flaked
2 Roma tomatoes, seeded and
  diced
Zest and juice of 1 lemon
Freshly ground black pepper
2 tablespoons roughly
  chopped cilantro

1. In a large bowl, rinse the rice several times with cold water. When the water is no longer cloudy, cover the rice with cold water and soak for about 10 minutes.

2. Bring a medium pot of water to a boil over high heat, then reduce the heat to medium-low, so it maintains a simmer. Carefully lower the eggs into the simmering water using a slotted spoon and cook for 7 minutes. Prepare a bowl of ice water. When the eggs are done, transfer them immediately to the ice bath.

3. While the rice is soaking, in a medium Dutch oven, melt the butter over medium heat and sauté the shallot with a pinch of salt for about 2 minutes, or until tender. Add the curry powder and sauté for a few seconds more, until the curry powder is fragrant.

Continued on next page ⟶

4. Drain the rice in a sieve and add to the pan. Fry for about 1 minute, making sure the rice grains are coated with the butter and spices.

5. Add the stock and another pinch of salt and cover. Cook for 2 minutes, then remove the pan from the heat and set aside, covered, for 10 minutes.

6. Remove the lid and add the mackerel, tomatoes, and lemon zest, gently folding the ingredients together. Season lightly with salt and pepper. Transfer the mixture to a warmed serving platter. Peel the eggs, halve them, and place them on top of the mackerel mixture. Top with the cilantro and a drizzle of the lemon juice.

TIP

Add smoked sardines or hot smoked salmon to this dish. If you're not into cilantro, replace it with a handful of chopped mint leaves for a burst of fresh flavor.

Tilapia in Green Curry

SERVES 4

PREP TIME:
15 minutes

COOK TIME:
35 minutes

ONE POT

This tilapia is perfumed with coconut milk and curry spices and will fill your kitchen with decadent aromas.

2 tablespoons coconut oil
1 large shallot, finely chopped
2½ tablespoons Thai green curry paste
1 (15-ounce) can full-fat coconut milk
¼ cup low-sodium vegetable stock
2 teaspoons fish sauce
Kosher salt
Freshly ground black pepper

4 (6-ounce) tilapia fillets
2 scallions, white and green parts, thinly sliced, for garnish
2 tablespoons shredded Thai basil, for garnish (about 8 leaves)
1 lime, cut into wedges, for garnish
Cooked rice, for serving

TIP

~~~

Use red or yellow curry paste for a milder curry.

1. Preheat the oven to 350°F.

2. Heat a large oven-safe skillet over medium-high heat. Add the coconut oil and swirl to coat. Once the oil is melted, add the shallot and sauté for about 4 minutes, or until soft and translucent.

3. Add the green curry paste and stir to combine. Reduce the heat to medium-low and add the coconut milk. Simmer for 5 minutes, stirring occasionally.

4. Stir in the vegetable stock and fish sauce and lightly season with salt and pepper. Continue to simmer for 2 minutes.

5. Season both sides of the tilapia with salt and pepper and place the fish in the curry sauce. Transfer the pan to the oven. Bake, uncovered, for 25 minutes, or until the tilapia feels firm and flakes slightly when pushed with a fork.

6. Garnish with the scallions, basil, and lime wedges. Serve immediately with cooked rice.

Blackened Catfish

PREP TIME:
20 minutes

COOK TIME:
10 minutes

30 MINUTES
OR LESS

5-INGREDIENT

To get a good blackening on your fish, use a very hot cast-iron skillet or griddle. But beware: Blackening in a skillet can produce a lot of smoke. Unless you have an excellent vent hood exhaust system in your kitchen, it's best to use your outdoor grill to get the heat you want for this recipe.

4 (4- to 6-ounce) catfish fillets
½ cup peanut oil

2 tablespoons Cajun Spice
Blend (page 217)
2 teaspoons garlic salt

1. Prepare the grill with about 5 pounds of charcoal and heat until the coals are white, or preheat a gas grill to high. Place a cast-iron griddle or skillet over the coals or gas burner for 20 minutes, until it is very hot.

2. Meanwhile, coat the catfish fillets with the peanut oil, then sprinkle with the Cajun Spice Blend and garlic salt on both sides. Marinate for 20 minutes.

3. Place the fillets in the hot skillet and cook for 5 minutes, until white, then flip and cook for 5 minutes more, until flaky. Serve immediately.

TIP

You can prep this recipe the night before. Combine the peanut oil and Cajun Spice Blend in a large zip-top bag, then add the catfish fillets. Seal the bag tightly, toss the catfish in the mixture, and marinate overnight in the refrigerator. When you're ready to cook, heat the grill and pick up with step 3.

Broiled Halibut with Cilantro-Corn Salad

SERVES 4

PREP TIME:
15 minutes

COOK TIME:
10 minutes

30 MINUTES OR LESS

When cooked properly, halibut is a deliciously moist, tender, firm fish that requires little seasoning to shine. This nourishing, flavor-packed dinner comes together in less time than it takes to order and wait for takeout.

1 pound halibut fillets, skin-on, rinsed, and patted dry
¼ cup extra-virgin olive oil, plus more for the fish
Kosher salt
4 fresh corn ears, kernels cut from the cob
1 pint cherry tomatoes, halved
½ shallot, minced

¼ cup chopped fresh cilantro leaves, plus a few leaves for garnish
¼ cup freshly squeezed lime juice
1 teaspoon ground cumin
½ teaspoon ground coriander
2 avocados, peeled, pitted, halved, and cut into slices

1. Preheat the oven to broil.

2. Place the halibut on a broiler pan, skin-side down, and brush the top with oil. Sprinkle salt evenly over the top.

3. Roast for about 7 minutes, depending on the thickness of the fish, until the internal temperature reaches 145°F. When done, the fish should be opaque inside and flake easily with a fork.

4. While the fish cooks, in a large bowl, stir together the corn, tomatoes, shallot, cilantro, oil, lime juice, cumin, and coriander to combine. Season with salt. Divide the salad among four plates and arrange the avocado slices attractively over each salad.

5. Divide the halibut and serve alongside the salad.

TIP

Use cod or another firm whitefish in place of the halibut if you'd like. The preparation will be similar; simply adjust the timing as needed.

Sole Meunière

SERVES 4

PREP TIME:
5 minutes

COOK TIME:
15 minutes

30 MINUTES
OR LESS

5-INGREDIENT

This dish is probably the most classic sole dish of all time and is prepared as frequently in French homes as it is in Parisian restaurants. Meunière translates to "in the miller's wife style," referring to the flour dusted over the fish.

8 (3- to 4-ounce) sole fillets
Sea salt
Freshly ground black pepper
½ cup all-purpose flour
20 tablespoons (2½ sticks)
  unsalted butter, divided

1 tablespoon freshly
  squeezed lemon juice
2 tablespoons chopped fresh
  parsley

1. Preheat the oven to 300°F.
2. Lightly season the fillets on both sides with salt and pepper. Place the flour on a large dinner plate and dredge the sole in it, shaking off any excess.
3. Melt 8 tablespoons of butter until foamy in a large nonstick skillet over medium-high heat. Add half of the fillets and cook until golden brown, about 3 minutes. Flip the fillets over and cook until golden brown, about 2 minutes. Transfer the cooked fillets to a large plate and keep warm in the oven. Repeat with the remaining fillets and wipe the skillet clean with paper towels.
4. Melt the remaining 12 tablespoons of butter over medium heat in the same skillet and cook until nut brown, about 2 minutes. Immediately stir in the lemon juice and parsley.
5. Arrange 2 sole fillets on each of four dinner plates. Pour the butter sauce evenly over the sole and serve.

Garlicky White Wine–Steamed Clams

SERVES 4

PREP TIME:
10 minutes

COOK TIME:
15 minutes

ONE POT

30 MINUTES
OR LESS

White wine, aromatics, and briny steamed clams are a certified classic for a reason. Perfect for a date night or appetizer, these insanely delicious clams scream to be sopped up with tons of crusty bread. That last bit is nonnegotiable.

1 loaf crusty French bread
3 tablespoons salted butter
3 tablespoons extra-virgin
   olive oil
1 large shallot, thinly sliced
8 garlic cloves, thinly sliced
½ teaspoon red pepper flakes

Pinch kosher salt
½ cup dry white wine
36 littleneck clams, scrubbed
   well
1 cup clam juice
¼ cup chopped fresh parsley
3 tablespoons minced chives

1. Preheat the oven to 425°F.

2. Cut the bread in half lengthwise. Spread the butter over the bread. Wrap the individual halves in aluminum foil and bake for 12 to 14 minutes, until golden brown.

3. In a large straight-sided sauté pan over medium heat, heat the olive oil. Add the shallot and cook until translucent, 2 to 3 minutes. Add the garlic, red pepper flakes, and salt. Sauté until the garlic is fragrant, about 30 seconds. Add the wine and cook for 1 minute more.

4. Add the clams and clam juice, cover, and steam for about 10 minutes, until the clams have opened. Discard any that do not open. Sprinkle with the parsley and chives and serve immediately with the crusty bread on the side.

Scallops Gratin

SERVES 4

PREP TIME:
15 minutes

COOK TIME:
15 minutes

This is a classic French seafood dish. Fresh sea scallops are poached, topped with a healthy spoonful of Mornay sauce, and then broiled until golden brown. You'll need four large scallop shells or small oven-safe gratin dishes for this recipe.

30 MINUTES OR LESS

1 tablespoon unsalted butter
1 shallot, finely diced
4 button mushrooms, finely diced
1 teaspoon chopped fresh thyme
2 tablespoons white wine, plus ½ cup

Sea salt
Freshly ground black pepper
1 pound sea scallops
1 recipe Mornay sauce (page 42)
4 tablespoons panko or regular bread crumbs

1. In a large skillet over medium-high heat, melt the butter until it is foamy. Add the shallot, mushrooms, thyme, and 2 tablespoons of wine and cook, stirring occasionally, until the shallot is soft, about 5 minutes. Season with salt and pepper to taste and spoon the mixture into the scallop shells or gratin dishes.

2. Preheat the oven to broil.

3. In a large saucepan over high heat, bring the remaining ½ cup of wine to a boil. Add the scallops and poach for 3 minutes, turning once. With a slotted spoon, remove the scallops and divide them evenly among the scallop shells or dishes.

4. Add the Mornay sauce to the cooking liquid and whisk together well. Spoon the sauce over the scallops and sprinkle each with 1 tablespoon of the bread crumbs. Broil until golden brown and bubbly, 6 to 7 minutes. Serve immediately.

TIP

If you're using shells, be sure to balance them on a small pile of coarse sea salt.

Mussels in Curried Coconut Milk

SERVES 4

PREP TIME:
5 minutes

COOK TIME:
15 minutes

ONE POT

30 MINUTES
OR LESS

This one-pot wonder is teeming with delicious aromatics like ginger, curry, coconut, and cilantro. Remember to serve big pieces of bread with this meal to soak up the exceptional sauce.

2 tablespoons extra-virgin olive oil
½ sweet onion, finely chopped
1 tablespoon minced garlic
2 teaspoons peeled and grated fresh ginger

1 tablespoon curry powder
1 cup full-fat coconut milk
1½ pounds fresh mussels, scrubbed and debearded
2 tablespoons finely chopped cilantro

1. Heat the olive oil in a large skillet over medium-high heat and sauté the onion, garlic, and ginger until softened, about 3 minutes.

2. Add the curry powder and toss to combine.

3. Stir in the coconut milk and bring to a boil.

4. Add the mussels, cover, and steam until the shells are open, about 8 minutes. Discard any unopened shells and remove the skillet from the heat.

5. Stir in the cilantro and serve.

TIP

*If you can't source
fresh mussels, buy
frozen ones and thaw
in the refrigerator
overnight.*

Piccata-Style Scallops

SERVES 4

PREP TIME:
5 minutes

The piccata process is beyond simple. Scallops get seared then dressed in a deliciously piquant, caper-studded pan sauce.

COOK TIME:
15 minutes

30 MINUTES OR LESS

½ cup all-purpose flour, for dredging
Kosher salt
Freshly ground black pepper
10 ounces (U10 or U12) scallops, side muscles removed and discarded
6 tablespoons (¾ stick) unsalted butter, divided

1 tablespoon extra-virgin olive oil
1 shallot, minced
½ cup dry white wine
¼ cup vegetable stock
3 tablespoons capers, drained
2 lemons, 1 for zest and juice, 1 cut into wedges
¼ cup chopped fresh parsley, plus more for garnish

1. Pour the flour in a shallow bowl and season with a pinch of salt and pepper.

2. Lightly dredge the scallops in the flour, shaking off any excess.

3. In a large skillet over medium-high heat, heat 2 tablespoons of butter and the olive oil. Once the skillet looks shimmery, place the scallops in the skillet, flat-side down, and cook, undisturbed, until golden brown, 3 to 4 minutes. Flip the scallops and cook for an additional 2 to 3 minutes. The sides of the scallops should be opaque. Transfer the scallops to a plate.

4. Spoon any excess oil out of the pan, if necessary, and melt 2 tablespoons of butter over medium-high heat. Once the butter is melted, add the shallot and sauté until translucent. Stir in the wine and a pinch of salt, deglazing the pan by scraping the bottom with a wooden spoon. Cook for about

2 minutes. Stir in the stock, capers, and lemon zest and cook for 1 minute more. Stir in ¼ cup of lemon juice and the remaining 2 tablespoons of butter. Taste and adjust the seasoning with salt and pepper. Stir in the parsley.

5. Return the scallops to the pan and spoon the sauce over them. Serve with a garnish of parsley and lemon wedges for squeezing.

TIP

Shrimp make a great substitute for scallops in this dish.

Cod and Potatoes in Avgolemono

SERVES 4

PREP TIME:
5 minutes

COOK TIME:
25 minutes

30 MINUTES OR LESS

If you've never had avgolemono, you're in for a treat. The tangy lemony broth pairs perfectly with the fish to create a flavor profile like no other. Buttery potatoes are cooked along with the fish, soaking up all the delightful avgolemono.

4 cups chicken broth
1 pound baby red potatoes, quartered
¼ cup chopped onion
3 garlic cloves, minced

Sea salt
Freshly ground black pepper
4 (5-ounce) cod fillets
2 large eggs
Juice of 1 lemon

1. In a large stockpot, bring the broth to a boil over high heat. Add the potatoes, onion, and garlic. Season with salt and pepper, cover, reduce the heat to low, and simmer for 15 minutes. Add the cod and simmer for 7 to 10 minutes more, until the fish is cooked through.

2. While the cod is simmering, in a small bowl, whisk together the eggs and lemon juice. While whisking continuously, slowly add 1 cup of the hot broth to the bowl with the egg mixture and whisk for a few seconds more to temper the egg mixture. Pour the mixture from the bowl back into the stockpot and stir to combine. Serve.

TIP

Make sure to temper the eggs because adding them directly to the pot with the hot broth will cause them to curdle. Store leftovers in an airtight container in the refrigerator for up to 3 days.

Fish and Chips

SERVES 4

PREP TIME:
10 minutes

COOK TIME:
35 minutes

This dish is a favorite in coastal shacks. This version with beer batter features a combination of two flours to create a slightly lighter texture. Homemade tartar sauce makes a perfect lemony, briny dipping sauce.

Olive oil, for brushing and drizzling

1½ pounds Yukon Gold potatoes, cut into ⅜-by-3-inch matchsticks

2 teaspoons kosher salt, plus more for seasoning

Freshly ground black pepper

1½ cups mayonnaise

2 tablespoons capers, drained, rinsed, and chopped

2 tablespoons chopped dill pickles

1 garlic clove, minced

Zest of 1 lemon

1 tablespoon freshly squeezed lemon juice

Avocado oil, for frying

1 cup rice flour

1 cup all-purpose flour

1 tablespoon baking powder

½ teaspoon Old Bay seasoning

1 (12-ounce) bottle lager beer

1½ pounds cod or haddock fillets, halved

Lemon wedges, for serving

Malt vinegar (optional)

1. Preheat the oven to 450°F. Brush a large baking sheet with olive oil.

2. Place the potatoes in a large pot and cover them with 2 inches of cold water. Set over medium-high heat, bring to a simmer, and cook the potatoes halfway through, about 5 minutes.

3. While the potatoes cook, place the prepared baking sheet in the oven to preheat.

4. Carefully drain the potatoes and place them on a layer of paper towels.

Continued on next page ⟶

TIP

~~~

Keep the fries warm in a 250°F oven while frying the cod fillets.

5. Spread the fries evenly on the baking sheet. Drizzle with olive oil and season with salt and pepper. Roast for 25 minutes, tossing after 10 minutes and again at the 20-minute mark.

6. In a small bowl, whisk together the mayonnaise, capers, pickles, garlic, lemon zest, and lemon juice. Cover with plastic wrap and store in the refrigerator until ready to serve.

7. In a large Dutch oven over medium heat, heat 3 inches of avocado oil to 350°F.

8. In a medium bowl, combine the rice flour, all-purpose flour, baking powder, 2 teaspoons of salt, and the Old Bay seasoning. Gradually pour in the beer while whisking constantly. Season the fish fillets with salt and pepper.

9. Dip the fillets in the batter and allow any excess to drip off.

10. Prepare a baking sheet or platter with paper towels. Fry the fillets for 4 to 5 minutes (depending on thickness), until golden brown and crispy. Transfer to the paper towel–lined baking sheet and season with salt.

11. Serve with the fries, tartar sauce, lemon wedges, and malt vinegar (if using).

Pistachio-Crusted Sea Bass

SERVES 4

PREP TIME:
10 minutes

COOK TIME:
30 minutes

30 MINUTES
OR LESS

Black sea bass fillets get a coating of flavorful sauce before being dipped in herbaceous pistachio crumbs and baked.

¾ cup pistachios, shelled
¼ cup panko bread crumbs
2 tablespoons chopped parsley
1 teaspoon lemon zest
2 teaspoons chopped thyme
½ teaspoon kosher salt, plus more for seasoning
½ teaspoon freshly ground black pepper, plus more for seasoning
2 tablespoons extra-virgin olive oil
1 small shallot, minced

2 garlic cloves, minced
1 small Fresno chile, seeded, pith removed, and minced
½ cup mayonnaise
1 large egg yolk
1 tablespoon Dijon mustard
1 teaspoon sriracha
1 teaspoon freshly squeezed lemon juice
Nonstick cooking spray
4 (6- to 8-ounce) black sea bass fillets, skinned and patted dry
Lemon wedges, for serving

1. Preheat the oven to 300°F.
2. In a food processor, combine the pistachios, bread crumbs, parsley, lemon zest, thyme, and a pinch of salt and pepper. Pulse until finely chopped.
3. Heat the olive oil in a large skillet over medium heat. Sauté the shallot until translucent, about 40 seconds. Add the garlic and chile and sauté until fragrant, 20 to 30 seconds.
4. Stir the shallot mixture into the pistachio crumbs and reserve in a shallow dish that is wide enough to fit the fillets in.
5. In a small bowl, whisk together the mayonnaise, egg yolk, Dijon mustard, sriracha, lemon juice, ½ teaspoon of salt, and

Continued on next page ⟶

½ teaspoon of pepper. Place in another shallow dish that is wide enough to fit the fillets in.

6. Set a wire rack atop a rimmed baking sheet and spray with nonstick spray. Dip the top of each fillet in the mayonnaise mixture, then in the pistachio crumbs, pressing down on the back of the fillet to make sure the bread crumbs adhere. Transfer the coated fillets to the greased wire rack atop the baking sheet.

7. Bake for 20 to 25 minutes, or until the fish is opaque throughout and flakes when gently poked with a paring knife.

8. Serve with lemon wedges.

Halibut en Papillote

SERVES 4

SERVES 4

PREP TIME:
10 minutes

COOK TIME:
10 minutes

30 MINUTES OR LESS

En papillote, or "in paper," is a great way to keep fish moist and a quick way to whip up a flavor-packed dinner on a whim. Buttery, briny Castelvetrano olives and punchy capers are combined with tomatoes, thyme, and garlic to create a delicious base for the lemon-topped halibut. The real magic of this dish happens when the white wine and tomatoes begin to create the flavor-packed steam in which the halibut cooks.

1 cup cherry tomatoes, halved lengthwise

1 cup Castelvetrano olives, roughly chopped

2 tablespoons capers, roughly chopped

4 garlic cloves, minced

2 tablespoons minced fresh thyme

4 tablespoons olive oil, plus more for drizzling

Kosher salt

Freshly ground black pepper

2 pounds halibut fillets, cut into 4 equal portions

1 lemon, sliced

4 tablespoons white wine

1. Preheat the oven to 400°F.

2. In a large bowl, mix the cherry tomatoes, olives, capers, garlic, and thyme. Give everything a generous drizzle of olive oil and a sprinkle of salt and pepper.

3. Prepare 4 large squares of parchment paper (one for each halibut fillet).

4. Spoon ¼ cup of the tomato mixture onto each square of parchment, then place a halibut fillet on top. Season each fillet with salt and pepper and drizzle each fillet with roughly 1 tablespoon of olive oil. Place 2 or 3 lemon slices on top of

Continued on next page ⟶

Halibut en Papillote continued

TIP

Cod is a great substitute for halibut in this dish.

each fillet and top with ¼ cup of the tomato mixture. Pour 1 tablespoon of wine on top of everything and fold the parchment into a tight package, making sure all edges are tightly crimped.

5. Bake for 10 minutes, or until the fish flakes when gently poked with a paring knife.

6. Serve in the packets.

Piccata-Style Monkfish

SERVES 2

PREP TIME:
10 minutes

COOK TIME:
10 minutes

30 MINUTES OR LESS

Monkfish gets seared to a perfectly golden exterior, then topped with a deliciously bright pan sauce of white wine, lemon, briny capers, and shallots. It is delightfully simple and positively decadent served alongside buttery mashed potatoes or a Parmigiano risotto.

2 (6-ounce) monkfish
fillets, about 1 inch thick,
membrane and skin
removed
Kosher salt
Freshly ground black pepper
¾ cup all-purpose flour
6 tablespoons (¾ stick)
unsalted butter, divided

3 tablespoons extra-virgin
olive oil
1 small shallot, minced
½ cup white wine
⅓ cup freshly squeezed
lemon juice
¼ cup capers, drained
¼ cup chopped fresh parsley
1 teaspoon lemon zest
Lemon wedges, for serving

1. Pat the monkfish fillets dry and season with salt and pepper.

2. Place the flour in a shallow dish and season it with salt and pepper. Lightly dredge the fillets in the flour, shaking off the excess.

3. In a large skillet over medium-high heat, melt 2 tablespoons of butter along with the olive oil. Cook the fillets for 2 to 3 minutes per side, until the internal temperature registers 130°F. Transfer the fish to a baking sheet to rest.

4. Add the shallot to the skillet, sautéing until translucent, about 1 minute. Pour in the wine and lemon juice and bring to a boil, making sure to scrape all the flavorful bits off the bottom of

Continued on next page ⟶

the skillet. Add the capers, parsley, and lemon zest. Turn off the heat and stir in the remaining 4 tablespoons of butter until nice and glossy. Taste for seasoning and adjust accordingly with salt and pepper.

5. Add the monkfish fillets to the skillet and baste with the piccata sauce. Plate and spoon extra sauce over the fillets. Serve with extra lemon wedges.

TIP

This sauce is so versatile; you can turn almost any protein into a piccata-style experience. Simply replicate the searing technique on your preferred seafood, such as scallops or shrimp, adjusting cook times as necessary, and make the pan sauce as directed here.

Broiled Arctic Char with Chimichurri

SERVES 6

PREP TIME:
20 minutes

COOK TIME:
5 minutes

30 MINUTES
OR LESS

Buttery arctic char fillets get marinated in a tangy lemon-Dijon vinaigrette before they are broiled and served alongside an herbaceous, bright chimichurri sauce.

¾ cup extra-virgin olive oil, divided, plus more for brushing
6 (4-ounce) arctic char fillets
Kosher salt
Freshly ground black pepper
¼ cup freshly squeezed lemon juice
1 tablespoon Dijon mustard
2 tablespoons minced chives
2 teaspoons lemon zest, divided

½ teaspoon honey
¾ cup finely chopped fresh parsley
2 red serrano chiles or Anaheim chiles, seeded, pith removed, and minced
4 garlic cloves, minced
2 tablespoons red wine vinegar
Lemon wedges, for serving

1. Position an oven rack 3 inches from the top and preheat the oven to broil. Brush a baking sheet with oil.

2. Season the arctic char fillets with salt and pepper.

3. In a small bowl, whisk together the lemon juice, Dijon, chives, 1 teaspoon of lemon zest, and the honey. Slowly stream in ¼ cup of olive oil while whisking constantly. Season with salt and pepper to taste. Place the fillets in a large zip-top bag, pour in the marinade, and refrigerate while making the chimichurri.

4. In a small bowl, combine the parsley, chiles, garlic, and red wine vinegar. Slowly stream in the remaining ½ cup of olive oil while whisking constantly. Season with salt and pepper. Taste and adjust as needed with salt, pepper, and extra red wine vinegar.

Continued on next page ⟶

TIP

Chimichurri can be made a day in advance and stored in an airtight jar in the refrigerator.

5. Remove the fillets from the marinade, allowing any excess to drip off. Place the fillets skin-side down on the prepared baking sheet. Broil for 5 minutes, or until the fish is opaque and flakes when poked gently with a paring knife. Transfer the fillets to a serving tray and spoon the chimichurri over the top.

6. Serve with lemon wedges and extra chimichurri sauce.

Parmigiano-Crusted Flounder

SERVES 4

PREP TIME:
10 minutes

COOK TIME:
20 minutes

30 MINUTES
OR LESS

Parmigiano is the ideal coating for flounder fillets with its salty, nutty goodness. Laced with lemon, garlic, and chives, this dish is the perfect weeknight wonder.

2 tablespoons extra-virgin olive oil, plus more for brushing
¾ cup grated Parmigiano-Reggiano cheese
¼ cup Italian bread crumbs
4 garlic cloves, minced

2 tablespoons minced chives, plus more for serving
1 teaspoon lemon zest, plus lemon wedges for serving
Kosher salt
Freshly ground black pepper
1 cup all-purpose flour
4 (8-ounce) flounder fillets
2 large eggs

1. Preheat the oven to 425°F. Line a large baking sheet with parchment paper and brush it with olive oil.

2. In a shallow baking dish, combine the Parmigiano-Reggiano cheese, bread crumbs, garlic, chives, lemon zest, and a pinch of salt and pepper. In another dish, combine the flour and a pinch of salt and pepper.

TIP

Serve with a peppery arugula salad dressed with lemon juice, olive oil, flaky salt, and pepper for a quick and healthy, Milanese-style dinner.

3. Season the flounder fillets with salt and pepper. Whisk the eggs in a small bowl and season with salt and pepper.

4. Dip the flounder first in the flour, then in the eggs, then in the bread crumb mixture, shaking off any excess. Gently press the bread crumbs into the flounder to help them adhere.

5. Place the fillets on the prepared baking sheet and drizzle each with about ½ tablespoon of oil. Bake for 20 minutes, or until golden brown.

6. Serve topped with extra chives and lemon wedges on the side.

6

SPECIAL OCCASIONS

Steamed Whole Whitefish with Sizzling Ginger Oil

SERVES 4

PREP TIME:
10 minutes

COOK TIME:
20 minutes

Virtually any whitefish has potential to be cooked whole— sea bass, red snapper, yellowtail snapper, rockfish, trout, or halibut. When buying a whole fish from the market, ask the fishmonger to clean it for you so it's ready to go as soon as you get it home. For a dash of spice, add slivers of thinly sliced fresh chiles to the sauce.

FOR THE FISH

1 whole whitefish (about 2 pounds), head-on and cleaned

½ cup kosher salt

3 scallions, white and green parts, sliced into 3-inch pieces

4 peeled fresh ginger slices, each about the size of a quarter

2 tablespoons Shaoxing rice wine

FOR THE SAUCE

2 tablespoons light soy sauce

1 tablespoon sesame oil

2 teaspoons sugar

FOR THE SIZZLING GINGER OIL

3 tablespoons avocado oil

2 tablespoons julienned peeled fresh ginger

2 scallions, white and green parts, thinly sliced

TO MAKE THE FISH

1. Rub the fish inside and out with the kosher salt. Rinse the fish and pat it dry with paper towels.

Continued on next page ⟶

2. On a plate that will fit into a bamboo steamer basket, make a bed using half of the scallions and half of the ginger. Lay the fish on top and stuff the remaining scallions and ginger inside the fish. Pour the rice wine over the fish.

3. Rinse a bamboo steamer basket and its lid under cold water and place it in a wok. Pour in about 2 inches of cold water, or until the water comes above the bottom rim of the steamer by ¼ to ½ inch, but not so high that the water touches the bottom of the basket. Bring the water to a boil.

4. Place the plate in the steamer basket and cover. Steam the fish over medium heat for 15 minutes (add 2 minutes for every additional ½ pound). Before removing it from the wok, poke the fish with a fork near the head. If the flesh flakes, it's done. If the flesh still sticks together, steam for 2 minutes more.

TO MAKE THE SAUCE

5. While the fish is steaming, in a small pan, warm the soy sauce, sesame oil, and sugar over low heat and set aside.

6. Once the fish is cooked, transfer it to a clean platter. Discard the cooking liquid and aromatics from the steaming plate. Pour the warm soy sauce mixture over the fish. Tent the fish with foil to keep it warm while you prepare the oil.

TO MAKE THE SIZZLING GINGER OIL

7. In a small saucepan, heat the avocado oil over medium heat. Just before it starts to smoke, add half of the ginger and half of the scallions and fry for 10 seconds. Pour the hot sizzling oil over the top of the fish.

8. Garnish with the remaining ginger and scallions and serve immediately.

Mackerel Piperade

SERVES 4

PREP TIME:
10 minutes

COOK TIME:
30 minutes

Mackerel is a great alternative to the cod in this piperade.

4 (6-ounce) mackerel fillets, skinned and pin bones removed
Kosher salt
Freshly ground black pepper
6 tablespoons extra-virgin olive oil, divided, plus more for garnish
1 medium white onion, cut into ½-inch strips
1 red bell pepper, seeded and cut into ½-inch strips
1 green bell pepper, seeded and cut into ½-inch strips
2 garlic cloves, minced
1 tablespoon smoked paprika
Pinch cayenne pepper
1 (14-ounce) can fire-roasted diced tomatoes, undrained
1 cup halved pitted green olives
2 tablespoons coarsely chopped fresh flat-leaf parsley, for garnish

1. Season the fillets with salt and pepper and drizzle 2 tablespoons of olive oil over the fish. Set aside on a plate.

2. In a large, wide sauté pan or skillet, heat the remaining 4 tablespoons of olive oil over medium-high heat. Add the onion, red pepper, and green pepper and cook until tender, about 7 minutes. Season with salt and pepper.

3. Add the garlic, paprika, and cayenne pepper and sauté for 1 minute, until the garlic is fragrant.

4. Add the tomatoes with their juices and stir gently to combine. Season with salt and pepper and add the olives. Reduce the heat to medium and simmer for 5 minutes.

5. Place the mackerel in the sauce and simmer, covered, for 10 minutes.

6. Serve hot, garnished with the parsley.

TIP

You can make a very hearty breakfast fish here by simmering a couple of cracked eggs in the piperade and stirring in some flaked smoked mackerel toward the end.

TIP

Use a wide sauté pan to cook everything evenly and try not to mix too much after adding the rice—the crispy rice at the bottom of the pan, known as socarrat, is delicious.

Seafood Paella

SERVES 4

PREP TIME:
10 minutes

COOK TIME:
45 minutes

A beloved regional Spanish staple, the mixture of rice, spice, and seafood works wonderfully well. Saffron and paprika add a lovely complex flavor and give the rice its trademark reddish tint.

1 tablespoon olive oil
8 ounces chicken andouille
  sausage links, sliced
1 small onion, diced
4 garlic cloves, minced
1 (12-ounce) can roasted red
  bell peppers, drained and
  chopped
1 (15-ounce) can diced
  tomatoes, drained
2 cups uncooked arborio rice
1 teaspoon paprika
½ teaspoon ground turmeric
Pinch saffron threads
Sea salt

Freshly ground black pepper
4 cups chicken broth
½ teaspoon red pepper flakes
1½ to 2 pounds mussels,
  scrubbed and debearded
1 pound littleneck clams,
  soaked for at least
  20 minutes and scrubbed
1 pound large (U31/40)
  shrimp, tail-on, peeled, and
  deveined
½ cup frozen peas
¼ cup chopped fresh Italian
  parsley
Lemon wedges, for serving

1. In a large sauté pan, heat the olive oil over medium heat. Add the sausage and cook for 3 to 5 minutes. Add the onion, garlic, and roasted red peppers and sauté for about 5 minutes. Add the tomatoes and cook for 1 to 2 minutes to blend the ingredients.

2. Add the rice and sauté for 1 minute. Add the paprika, turmeric, and saffron and season with salt and black pepper. Sauté for 1 minute. Add the broth and red pepper flakes and increase the heat to medium-high to bring the mixture to a boil. Reduce

Continued on next page ⟶

the heat to low, cover, and simmer for 20 minutes, or until the liquid has been almost completely absorbed.

3. Add the mussels, clams, shrimp, and peas. Cover and increase the heat to medium. Cook for 7 to 10 minutes, until the seafood is just cooked through. (Discard any clams or mussels that do not open after 10 minutes of cooking.)

4. Garnish with the parsley and serve with lemon wedges.

Caramel Simmered Catfish (Cá Kho Tộ)

SERVES 4

PREP TIME:
10 minutes

COOK TIME:
35 minutes

This Vietnamese recipe is traditionally cooked in a clay pot, but a little-known restaurant secret about this dish is that they only serve the dish in a clay pot at the table. Most of the time, it's cooked in conventional saucepans back in the kitchen.

2 catfish fillets (about 1 pound), cut into 4 equal pieces

1 teaspoon Chinese five-spice powder

1 tablespoon fish sauce

Kosher salt

Freshly ground black pepper

2 tablespoons avocado oil

1 small shallot, thinly sliced

4 garlic cloves, thinly sliced

1 red Fresno chile, thinly sliced

1 cup coconut water

¼ cup sugar

2 tablespoons water

Juice of 1 lime, for garnish

1 tablespoon chopped fresh cilantro, for garnish

Steamed rice, for serving

1. Pat the catfish dry with paper towels and place it in a bowl. Season with the five-spice powder, fish sauce, salt, and pepper. Marinate for 5 to 10 minutes.

2. In a nonstick skillet, heat the oil over medium-high heat. Add the shallot and garlic and sauté until browned, about 1 minute. Add the Fresno chile and sauté for 1 minute more.

3. Push the vegetables to the side of the pan and sear the catfish on both sides, about 3 minutes per side, until golden brown. Add the coconut water and reduce the heat to medium-low. Braise the fish in the simmering coconut water while you prepare the sauce.

Continued on next page ⟶

Caramel Simmered Catfish (Cá Kho Tộ) continued

Caramel Simmered Catfish (Cá Kho Tộ) continued

TIP

Tilapia is a good substitute for catfish in this recipe.

4. In a small saucepan or nonstick skillet, heat the sugar and water over medium-high heat until the mixture starts to bubble and caramelize, about 6 to 7 minutes. Immediately pour it over the fish.

5. Simmer the fish in the caramel sauce for 20 minutes, or until the sauce thickens and the fish has taken on a deep caramelized color.

6. Transfer the fish and sauce to bowls. Garnish with the lime juice and cilantro. Serve with steamed rice.

Whole Fried Snapper

SERVES 4

PREP TIME:
15 minutes

COOK TIME:
10 minutes

A visually showstopping dish, whole red snapper gets fried to light, crispy perfection. It's then topped with an herbaceous, Thai-inspired vinaigrette of cilantro, shallots, chiles, and lime to cut through all of that richness.

2 red serrano chiles, thinly sliced

4 garlic cloves, grated

1 (2-inch) piece fresh ginger, peeled and minced

1 cup roughly chopped fresh cilantro

¼ cup lime juice, plus wedges for serving

1½ tablespoons fish sauce

1 tablespoon red wine vinegar

1 tablespoon honey

2 shallots, thinly sliced

¼ cup extra-virgin olive oil

Kosher salt

Freshly ground black pepper

1 whole red snapper (2 to 2½ pounds), cleaned and scaled

½ cup all-purpose flour

Avocado oil, for frying

4 scallions, white and green parts, thinly sliced, for serving

1. In a food processor, combine the chiles, garlic, and ginger and pulse until paste-like. Scrape down the sides with a spatula and transfer to a small bowl. Add the cilantro, lime juice, fish sauce, vinegar, honey, and shallots. While whisking, stream in the olive oil. Season with salt and pepper to taste. Refrigerate until ready to serve.

2. Cut 3 slashes in the thickest part of the snapper on each side. Season all over with salt and pepper.

3. Place the flour on a large plate and season with salt and pepper. Lightly dredge the fish in the flour, shaking off any excess.

Continued on next page ⟶

TIP

You can also do a whole branzino here instead of the snapper.

4. Set a large cast-iron skillet over medium heat. Fill it one-third full of avocado oil and heat the oil to 350°F. Fry the snapper until golden and crispy, 4 to 5 minutes per side. Transfer to a paper towel–lined plate to drain excess oil.

5. Place the snapper on a serving platter and top with the chile-ginger vinaigrette and scallions.

6. Serve with the lime wedges.

Shrimp Creole

SERVES 6

PREP TIME:
30 minutes

**COOK
TIME:** 1 hour
15 minutes

Shrimp get simmered in a flavorful tomato sauce for this southern Louisiana classic. Shrimp are a locally sourced ingredient in that region, making them prevalent in many Creole and Cajun dishes.

2 tablespoons unsalted butter
½ cup chopped onion
½ cup chopped celery
½ cup chopped bell peppers (any color)
2 tablespoons minced garlic
2 tablespoons all-purpose flour
1½ quarts seafood or chicken stock
2 (14-ounce) cans diced tomatoes, undrained
1 (16-ounce) jar tomato-based chili sauce

1 teaspoon dried thyme
1 bay leaf
½ teaspoon cayenne pepper
½ teaspoon Worcestershire sauce
2⅔ cups water
1⅓ cups converted rice
⅓ teaspoon kosher salt, plus more for seasoning
1½ pounds shrimp, tail-off, peeled, and deveined
Freshly ground black pepper

1. In a large saucepan over medium-high heat, melt the butter. Add the onion, celery, and bell peppers and cook for about 5 minutes, stirring, until soft. Stir in the garlic and cook for about 1 minute, until aromatic. Add the flour and cook for about 5 minutes, stirring frequently with a wooden spoon to keep the flour from burning. Add the stock and mix well until the sauce has a smooth consistency.

2. Stir in the tomatoes with their juices, chili sauce, thyme, bay leaf, cayenne pepper, and Worcestershire sauce and bring to a boil. Turn the heat down to low and simmer, uncovered, for 1 hour, stirring often to prevent scorching.

Continued on next page ⟶

3. About 30 minutes before serving, make the rice. In a medium saucepan over high heat, bring the water to a boil. Stir in the rice and salt, turn the heat down to low, cover, and simmer for about 25 minutes, until the rice is tender and the liquid is absorbed. Remove from the heat.

4. Stir the shrimp into the tomato mixture and cook for about 5 minutes, until the shrimp turn pink. Season with salt and pepper to taste. Serve the shrimp over the rice and have plenty of hot sauce available.

Crab Spaghetti

SERVES 4

PREP TIME:
10 minutes

COOK TIME:
10 minutes

Luxurious lump crabmeat gets tossed with perfectly al dente spaghetti in a rich, slightly spicy, garlicky pan sauce.

1 pound spaghetti
4 tablespoons (½ stick)
  unsalted butter, divided
2 tablespoons extra-virgin
  olive oil
7 garlic cloves, thinly sliced
2 small red serrano or Fresno
  chiles, seeded, pith removed,
  and minced
1 teaspoon roughly chopped
  thyme

2 teaspoons lemon zest,
  divided
Kosher salt
Freshly ground black pepper
¼ cup freshly squeezed
  lemon juice
1 pound fresh lump crabmeat
Parmigiano-Reggiano cheese,
  freshly grated, for serving

TIP

Chunks of lobster meat or even shrimp would be a delicious swap for crab.

1. Bring a large pot of salted water to a rolling boil over high heat. Cook the spaghetti until just barely shy of al dente, about 7 to 8 minutes. Reserve ½ cup of pasta water, drain the pasta, and set it aside.

2. In a large sauté pan, heat 2 tablespoons of butter and the olive oil over medium heat. Add the garlic, chiles, thyme, and 1 teaspoon of lemon zest. Season with salt and pepper. Sauté until fragrant, about 1 minute.

3. Add the lemon juice and the remaining butter. Stir until the butter is emulsified into the sauce. Season with salt and pepper to taste. Add the pasta and the crabmeat. Toss to combine until the crab is warmed through, adding pasta water as needed to help the sauce emulsify.

4. Transfer to shallow serving bowls, top with the Parmigiano-Reggiano cheese, remaining 1 teaspoon of lemon zest, and plenty of black pepper.

Shrimp Mozambique

SERVES 4 TO 6

PREP TIME: 20 minutes

COOK TIME: 30 minutes

2 pounds medium (U41/50) "easy-peel" shrimp, tail-on and deveined

1 teaspoon kosher salt, divided, plus more for seasoning

¼ cup extra-virgin olive oil

1 large onion, quartered and sliced

2 tablespoons salted butter

8 garlic cloves, sliced

2 packets azafrán seasoning or 5 or 6 saffron tendrils

1 (12-ounce) lager beer

¼ cup chopped fresh flat-leaf parsley

1 tablespoon Pimenta Moida (page 218)

1 teaspoon piri piri or other hot sauce

½ teaspoon Portuguese Allspice (page 219) or paprika

Juice of 1 lemon

3 cups water, divided

1 teaspoon cornstarch

3 or 4 lemon slices, for garnish

3 or 4 parsley sprigs, for garnish

1. Place the shrimp on a plate and sprinkle with ½ teaspoon of kosher salt.

2. In a large stockpot, heat the olive oil over medium heat. Add the onion and butter and cook until soft, about 10 minutes. Sprinkle with a pinch of salt. Add the garlic and cook for 1 minute. Add the azafrán seasoning and stir to combine.

3. Pour the beer into the pot and deglaze by scraping the bottom of the pot with a wooden spoon. Add the parsley, Pimenta Moida, piri piri, allspice, and lemon juice and stir to combine. Raise the heat to medium-high, stir in 2 cups of water, and bring to a simmer. Reduce the heat to medium, add the shrimp, and cook until they turn pink, 5 to 10 minutes.

4. In a medium bowl, whisk the remaining 1 cup of water and the cornstarch. Add to the stockpot and cook, stirring frequently, for 5 minutes.

5. Garnish with the lemon slices and parsley sprigs and serve.

Seared Scallops with Pineapple Beurre Blanc

SERVES 4

PREP TIME:
10 minutes

COOK TIME:
30 minutes

A pineapple version of classic beurre blanc brings out the inherent sweetness in scallops. An unexpected take, this bright and buttery sauce manages to cut through the richness of the scallops while still letting them shine.

FOR THE BEURRE BLANC SAUCE

1 large shallot, minced
½ cup white wine vinegar
½ cup pineapple juice
½ cup white wine, such as
  sauvignon blanc

2 cups (4 sticks) unsalted
  butter, cut into ½-inch cubes
  and chilled

FOR THE SCALLOPS

12 jumbo (U/15) scallops
Kosher salt
Freshly ground black pepper
3 tablespoons ghee or
  clarified butter

Ice water, if needed
2 tablespoons thinly sliced
  chives

TO MAKE THE BEURRE BLANC SAUCE

1. In a medium skillet, combine the shallot, vinegar, pineapple juice, and white wine. Bring to a boil over high heat, then reduce the heat to medium. Simmer for 15 to 20 minutes, or until the liquid has reduced to about 2 tablespoons.

2. Increase the heat to medium-high. Remove the butter from the refrigerator and add a few cubes at a time, whisking vigorously. As the butter melts, it should take on a velvety texture while being whisked. When you have 3 or 4 pieces of butter remaining, take the pan off the heat and stir in the last pieces until incorporated. Set aside and keep warm, but not hot.

TO MAKE THE SCALLOPS

3. Heat a cast-iron skillet over medium-high heat. Blot the scallops dry with a paper towel and season both sides with salt and pepper. As soon as the skillet starts to smoke, add the ghee and swirl quickly to coat the pan.

4. Add the scallops to the pan in a clockwise pattern, starting at 12 o'clock, so they cook for the same amount of time before you flip them. Sear for 3 minutes per side, or until they develop a deep-seared crust. Transfer the scallops to a plate and tent with foil.

5. Reheat the beurre blanc sauce over medium-high heat, whisking vigorously until warm again. Do not overheat, or the sauce will separate. If that happens, quickly whisk in ice water, 1 tablespoon at a time, until the sauce comes back together.

6. Plate by spooning generous amounts of sauce on the bottoms of warmed serving plates and arranging 3 scallops per plate. Garnish with the chives and serve hot.

TIP

Beurre blanc is a delicate emulsion of melted butter and concentrated vinegar and wine. Classic preparations strain out the shallots after reducing, but the little bits have great texture. Use this sauce with any pan-seared or broiled fish. A classic beurre blanc reduces white wine vinegar and white wine, but feel free to play with different vinegars, wines, and fruit juices to create your signature sauce.

Lobster Mac and Cheese

**SERVES
6 TO 8**

PREP TIME:
30 minutes,
plus
40 minutes
to chill

**COOK
TIME:** 1 hour
5 minutes

If you are craving comfort food but are also feeling spendy, take this recipe for a spin! It takes extra work, but the results are worth it. This recipe calls for live lobsters, but if you'd rather not cook them, that's okay. Simply buy cooked lobster—it'll still be great, and you'll save some time.

2 (2-pound) live lobsters or 1½ pounds cooked lobster meat
½ cup kosher salt, divided, plus more for seasoning
1 quart whole milk
12 tablespoons (1½ sticks) unsalted butter, divided
1 pound dried cavatappi pasta

1½ cups panko bread crumbs
½ cup all-purpose flour
Pinch cayenne pepper
1 tablespoon Dijon mustard
4 cups grated Gruyère cheese
2 cups grated sharp cheddar cheese
2 tablespoons roughly chopped fresh parsley

1. Fill a large bowl with ice water and set it aside.

2. Use the tip of a very sharp and heavy chef's knife to dispatch the lobsters. Drive the tip straight into the crack on the head, behind the eyes.

3. Bring a large stockpot of water to a rolling boil and add ¼ cup of salt. Lower the lobsters into the water and cook until they turn bright red, about 5 to 7 minutes.

4. Use kitchen tongs to lift the lobsters from the pot and immediately plunge them into the ice water. Chill for 10 minutes, then drain.

5. When the lobsters are cold, remove the tails and claws and discard the bodies (or use for another recipe). Crack the shells from the tails and claws and remove the meat, reserving the shells. Trim out the vein that runs down the tail and cut the

meat into ½-inch chunks. Place the meat in a strainer set over a bowl to catch the excess liquid and chill in the refrigerator for at least 30 minutes.

TIP

Break up the recipe into smaller do-ahead chunks. Cook and shell the lobster a couple of days in advance. Simmer the milk and cook the pasta ahead, too. Assemble everything the day you want to serve it, and serve it hot, right from the oven.

6. Preheat the oven to 375°F.

7. In a large saucepan over medium heat, simmer the milk and lobster shells together for 10 to 12 minutes. Butter the bottom and sides of a deep 3-quart casserole dish with 2 tablespoons of butter. Set aside.

8. Fill the stockpot with fresh water and bring it to a boil over high heat. Add the remaining ¼ cup of salt and cook the pasta according to the package directions. Drain and set aside.

9. Return the stockpot to the stove and melt the remaining 10 tablespoons of butter over medium heat. Remove 2 tablespoons of melted butter and stir it into a small bowl along with the bread crumbs, then set aside. Whisk the flour and cayenne pepper into the butter in the stockpot. Continue stirring until the flour begins to smell nutty, about 2 to 3 minutes. Stir in the Dijon mustard and season with a generous pinch of salt.

10. Strain the milk directly into the stockpot and discard the lobster shells. Increase the heat to medium-high and continue whisking as the sauce comes to a boil; it will become smooth and thick in 5 to 7 minutes. Stir in the Gruyère cheese, cheddar cheese, and cooked pasta. Taste and add more salt if needed. Fold in the chopped lobster and transfer to the baking dish.

11. Stir the parsley and a pinch of salt into the bread crumbs and sprinkle it all over the top of the mac and cheese. Bake for 20 to 25 minutes, or until the mac and cheese is bubbly and the bread crumbs have browned. Remove it from the oven and let it sit for 5 to 10 minutes before serving.

Moules Frites

SERVES 4

PREP TIME:
20 minutes

COOK TIME:
30 minutes

Moules frites, aka mussels and fries, are a match made in heaven. Briny mussels get steamed in a garlicky, herbaceous, boozy broth, then paired with crispy, creamy rosemary fries made effortlessly in the oven.

3 tablespoons extra-virgin olive oil, divided, plus more for brushing

1½ pounds Yukon Gold potatoes, cut into ⅜-by-3-inch matchsticks

1 tablespoon chopped fresh rosemary

Kosher salt

Freshly ground black pepper

2 pounds mussels

1 cup mayonnaise

8 garlic cloves, minced, divided

½ tablespoon freshly squeezed lemon juice

1 teaspoon lemon zest

4 tablespoons (½ stick) unsalted butter, divided

2 shallots, minced

1 red serrano or Fresno chile, seeded, pith removed, and minced

1 cup dry marsala wine

2 teaspoons chopped fresh thyme

¼ cup roughly chopped fresh parsley

1. Preheat the oven to 450°F. Brush a large baking sheet with oil.

2. Add the potatoes to a large stockpot and cover them with cold water. Bring to a simmer over medium-high heat. Cook the potatoes halfway through, about 5 minutes. While they cook, place the prepared baking sheet in the oven to preheat. Carefully drain the potatoes on a layer of paper towels.

3. Spread the potatoes evenly across the hot baking sheet. Drizzle with 2 tablespoons of olive oil, then sprinkle with the rosemary and a generous pinch of salt and pepper. Roast for 25 minutes, tossing after 10 minutes and again at the 20-minute mark.

4. In a medium bowl, soak the mussels in ice-cold water for about 15 minutes to purge them of any sand. Pick them out individually when done. Debeard if not done so already. Discard any that are not completely shut.

5. In a small bowl, whisk together the mayonnaise, half of the garlic, the lemon juice, lemon zest, and a pinch of salt and pepper. Set aside.

6. In a large sauté pan over medium heat, combine 2 tablespoons of butter and the remaining 1 tablespoon of olive oil. Once the butter melts, add the shallots and sauté for about 1 minute. Add the chile and remaining garlic, sautéing until fragrant, about 20 seconds. Add the marsala, thyme, and remaining 2 tablespoons of butter. Season with salt and pepper. Gently add the mussels, tossing everything in the pan to evenly coat with the marsala mixture. Cover and steam, shaking the pan occasionally to redistribute the mussels, 5 to 7 minutes. Discard any mussels that have not opened.

7. Spoon into serving bowls, top with the parsley, and serve with the rosemary fries and garlic aioli.

TIP

This dish would also be delicious with clams instead of mussels. Begin checking clams after 5 minutes.

Whole Roasted Branzino with Citrus Salsa

SERVES 6

PREP TIME:
15 minutes

COOK TIME:
25 minutes

Roasted whole branzino is stuffed with lemon and aromatics before getting topped with lemony caper compound butter and roasted. As if that weren't delicious enough, a citrus salsa makes a beautifully bright topper to highlight the branzino's flavor.

1 orange
1 grapefruit
¼ cup chopped fresh dill, plus 2 tablespoons
3 tablespoons capers, roughly chopped, divided
1 garlic clove, minced
2 tablespoons extra-virgin olive oil, plus more for drizzling
Kosher salt
Freshly ground black pepper
12 tablespoons (1½ sticks) unsalted butter, divided, at room temperature

1 red serrano chile, seeded, pith removed, and minced
1 shallot, minced
1½ tablespoons freshly squeezed lemon juice
1 teaspoon lemon zest
3 (1-pound) whole branzino, scaled and gutted
3 large rosemary sprigs
3 large thyme sprigs
2 lemons, 1 thinly sliced into rounds

1. Preheat the oven to 425°F.

2. Cut the ends off of the orange and grapefruit. Place each fruit flat-side down on a cutting board. Remove the rind from the fruit. If some pith remains, use a paring knife to remove it. Observe where the fruit is separated by membranes into segments. Set each fruit on its side. Cut along a membrane toward the center, repeating the same technique with the adjacent membrane until the cuts meet, releasing the citrus segment.

Repeat with the remaining fruit until it is all divided into segments.

3. Combine the citrus segments in a bowl along with ¼ cup of dill, 1 tablespoon of capers, the garlic, and a generous drizzle of olive oil. Season with salt and pepper. Gently toss to combine. Cover and refrigerate.

4. In a small bowl, combine 6 tablespoons of butter, the chile, shallot, lemon juice, lemon zest, remaining 2 tablespoons of capers, and remaining 2 tablespoons of dill and mix well. Season with salt and pepper.

5. Season the branzino exterior and cavities with salt and pepper. Stuff 1 rosemary sprig, 1 thyme sprig, and 2 lemon slices in each.

6. In a large oven-safe skillet, heat 2 tablespoons of olive oil over high heat. Add the branzino, working in batches, and cook until the skin is browned and crisp, about 3 minutes per side. Transfer to a baking sheet and top each with 2 tablespoons of butter.

7. Roast for 10 to 12 minutes, until just cooked through.

8. Transfer the branzino to a serving plate. Add salt and pepper to taste and serve alongside the citrus salsa.

TIP

To supreme citrus is to remove the membrane from the fruit so it can be served in slices without the pith and rind. A sharp paring knife is your best friend for this task.

Parmigiano-Crusted Sole with Pesto Orzo

SERVES 4

PREP TIME:
20 minutes

COOK TIME:
20 minutes

Tender fillets of sole encrusted in salty Parmigiano-Reggiano cheese get served alongside orzo, a rice-shaped pasta, and tossed in a lemony, peppery arugula pesto.

¾ cup olive oil, plus ½ tablespoon, plus more for brushing

1 cup grated Parmigiano-Reggiano cheese, divided, plus more for serving

¼ cup Italian bread crumbs

2 teaspoons lemon zest, divided

7 garlic cloves, minced, divided

2 tablespoons minced chives, plus more for serving

Kosher salt

Freshly ground black pepper

1 cup all-purpose flour

2 large eggs

2 pounds sole fillets

1½ cups arugula

1 cup basil leaves

½ cup toasted pine nuts, divided

¼ cup freshly squeezed lemon juice

¼ teaspoon red pepper flakes

3 cups dried orzo

Lemon wedges, for serving

1. Preheat the oven to 425°F. Line a large baking sheet with parchment paper and brush with olive oil.

2. Bring a large pot of salted water to a rolling boil over high heat.

3. In a shallow dish, combine ¾ cup of the Parmigiano-Reggiano, the bread crumbs, 1 teaspoon of lemon zest, half of the garlic, the chives, and a pinch of salt and pepper. Stir to combine.

4. In another shallow dish, combine the flour with a pinch of salt and pepper.

5. In a small bowl, whisk the eggs and season with salt and pepper.

6. Dip the sole in the flour, then in the eggs, then in the bread crumb mixture, allowing any excess to drip off after each. Gently press the bread crumbs onto the sole to help them adhere.

7. Place the fillets on the prepared baking sheet and drizzle with ½ tablespoon of oil. Bake for 20 minutes, or until golden brown.

8. In the bowl of a food processor, put the remaining garlic, remaining 1 teaspoon of lemon zest, the arugula, basil, ⅓ cup of pine nuts, lemon juice, and red pepper flakes. Pulse to combine. Once the mixture is finely chopped, process again while slowly streaming in the remaining ¾ cup of olive oil. Add the remaining ¼ cup of Parmigiano-Reggiano and pulse to mix.

9. Cook the orzo in the boiling water according to the package directions until al dente. Transfer to a large serving bowl and toss with the pesto and remaining whole pine nuts.

10. Serve the sole topped with extra chives and Parmigiano-Reggiano alongside the pesto orzo with lemon wedges.

TIP

Tilapia or pollock would be a great substitute for sole.

Grilled Swordfish with Miso Compound Butter

SERVES 4

PREP TIME:
10 minutes

COOK TIME:
40 minutes

Umami-rich mushroom risotto pairs perfectly with meaty, grilled swordfish steaks topped with miso butter.

6 cups chicken stock
8 tablespoons (1 stick) unsalted butter, at room temperature, divided
2 tablespoons miso paste
1 teaspoon lemon zest
3 tablespoons extra-virgin olive oil, divided
1 pound cremini mushrooms, roughly chopped
Kosher salt
Freshly ground black pepper
1 yellow onion, finely diced

4 garlic cloves, minced
2½ teaspoons thyme, divided
1 cup arborio rice
½ cup white wine
4 (5- to 6-ounce) swordfish steaks
½ cup grated Parmigiano-Reggiano cheese, plus more for serving
¼ cup roughly chopped fresh parsley
Lemon wedges, for serving

1. In a large pot over medium-high heat, bring the stock to a simmer, then reduce the heat to medium-low and continue simmering.

2. Prepare a grill and bring the temperature to medium-high heat (400°F to 450°F).

3. In a small bowl, mix 4 tablespoons of butter, the miso paste, and lemon zest.

4. In a large saucepan, melt 2 tablespoons of butter and 2 tablespoons of oil over medium heat. Add the mushrooms and sauté until golden brown, about 5 minutes. Season with salt and pepper. Add the onion and sauté until translucent, about 1 minute. Add the garlic and thyme and sauté until fragrant, about 30 seconds. Add the rice and sauté until opaque, about 1 minute. Add the wine and allow it to reduce for 1 to 2 minutes.

5. Add enough stock to cover the rice and cook, stirring, until the rice has absorbed almost all of the stock. Repeat with ½-cup measures of stock until the rice is al dente, about 17 minutes. You will not use all of the stock. Remove the saucepan from the heat.

6. Brush the swordfish steaks with the remaining 1 tablespoon of olive oil and season generously with salt and pepper. Grill the fish until it lifts off the grates without sticking, 5 to 6 minutes per side. Top each steak with 1 tablespoon of miso butter. Cover with foil.

7. Place the rice back on low heat and stir ⅓ cup of warm stock into it. Stir in the remaining 2 tablespoons of butter. The risotto's texture should be al dente, not gummy. Stir in the Parmigiano-Reggiano cheese.

8. Spoon the risotto into shallow bowls and top with the grilled swordfish, parsley, and extra Parmigiano-Reggiano cheese. Serve with lemon wedges.

TIP

Spoon the miso butter onto plastic wrap and roll into a log for easy storing and cutting. The miso butter can be made a few days in advance.

Grilled Snapper with Lemony Risotto

SERVES 4

PREP TIME:
10 minutes

COOK TIME:
30 minutes

Arborio rice gets toasted along with onion and garlic before deglazing with wine and gradually simmering to silky perfection. Grilled snapper gets laid atop a bed of the creamy, lemony risotto for a luxuriously summery meal.

6 cups chicken stock

4 tablespoons (½ stick) unsalted butter, divided

4 tablespoons extra-virgin olive oil, divided

1 yellow onion, finely diced

4 garlic cloves, minced

Kosher salt

Freshly ground black pepper

1 cup arborio rice

½ cup white wine

2 teaspoons lemon zest

2 teaspoons thyme, divided

2½ pounds red snapper fillets

⅓ cup freshly squeezed lemon juice

½ cup Parmigiano-Reggiano cheese, plus more for serving

2 tablespoons chopped chives

2 tablespoons chopped fresh parsley

Lemon wedges, for serving

1. In a large pot over medium-high heat, bring the stock to a simmer, then reduce the heat to medium-low and continue simmering. Prepare a grill and bring the temperature to medium-high heat (400°F to 450°F).

2. In a large saucepan, melt 2 tablespoons of butter and 2 tablespoons of oil over medium heat. Add the onion and sauté until translucent, 1 to 2 minutes. Add the garlic, season with salt and pepper, and sauté until fragrant, about 30 seconds. Add the rice and sauté until opaque, about 1 minute. Add the wine, lemon zest, and thyme. Cook for 1 to 2 minutes to allow it to reduce.

3. Add enough stock to cover the rice, stirring, until the rice has absorbed almost all of the stock. Repeat using ½-cup measures of stock until the rice is al dente, about 17 minutes. You will not use all of the stock. Remove the saucepan from the heat.

4. Pat the snapper dry with paper towels and season with salt and pepper. Rub with the remaining 2 tablespoons of olive oil. Place the fish on the grill grate, skin-side down, and grill, undisturbed, until the flesh is opaque everywhere but the thickest part, 6 to 8 minutes. Turn the fillets with a fish spatula, being careful not to tear the skin. Grill for 1 minute.

5. Return the rice to low heat and stir in the lemon juice and ⅓ cup of hot stock. Stir in the remaining 2 tablespoons of butter. The texture of the risotto should be al dente, not gummy. Stir in the Parmigiano-Reggiano cheese and chives.

6. Spoon the risotto into shallow bowls and top with the grilled snapper, parsley, and extra Parmigiano-Reggiano. Serve with lemon wedges.

TIP

If the rice still seems a little underdone, keep adding stock and stirring to incorporate. For leftovers, next-day cold risotto makes excellent arancini (fried, bread crumb–coated risotto balls), which need to be chilled before forming and frying.

Pan-Seared Halibut with Tomato-Feta Vinaigrette

SERVES 4

PREP TIME:
10 minutes

COOK TIME:
50 minutes

Beautifully seared halibut gets paired with crispy, craggy-edged, rosemary-laced potatoes and topped with a perfectly punchy, garlicky vinaigrette studded with sweet tomatoes, fresh herbs, and salty feta.

4 tablespoons extra-virgin olive oil, divided, plus more for brushing and drizzling
½ pound baby potatoes
Kosher salt
2 tablespoons minced chives
1 tablespoon finely chopped fresh rosemary
Freshly ground black pepper
2½ cups cherry tomatoes, halved

½ cup roughly chopped fresh parsley
1 small shallot, minced
3 garlic cloves, minced
3 tablespoons red wine vinegar
⅓ cup feta, crumbled
4 halibut fillets (about 2½ pounds), skinned
1½ tablespoons unsalted butter

1. Preheat the oven to 450°F. Brush a large baking sheet with olive oil.

2. Put the potatoes in a large pot and cover them with 2 inches of cold water and a generous pinch of salt. Cover with a lid and bring to a simmer over medium-high heat. Cook until the potatoes are fork-tender, about 7 minutes. Drain, return to the pot, and cover until cool enough to handle, 3 to 5 minutes.

3. Place the potatoes on the prepared baking sheet and with the back of a fork, gently press each to flatten them out a bit. Space the flattened potatoes out into an even layer. Drizzle each with olive oil and season with the chives, rosemary, and salt and pepper to taste.

4. Roast for 20 minutes, flip with a metal spatula, and roast for 20 minutes more, or until very brown.

5. While the potatoes are cooking, in a medium bowl, mix the tomatoes, parsley, shallot, garlic, vinegar, and a pinch of salt and pepper. Add 2 tablespoons of olive oil and the feta. Refrigerate until ready to serve.

6. Heat the remaining 2 tablespoons of oil in a large skillet on medium-high. Add the fillets and cook for 5 minutes, until lightly golden brown. Add the butter to the pan, basting it over the halibut fillets until cooked, 2 minutes.

7. Transfer the fish to serving plates with the potatoes. Top with the tomato-feta vinaigrette and serve.

TIP

Cod or any firm whitefish fillet would work well in this dish.

7

ON THE GRILL

New Orleans–Style Barbecued Shrimp

SERVES 4

PREP TIME:
15 minutes

COOK TIME:
10 minutes

This is a deliciously simple dish full of complex flavors. Shrimp get grilled before getting tossed in a flavorful sauce of garlic, lemon, butter, Worcestershire, herbs, and spices.

4 tablespoons (½ stick) unsalted butter

¼ cup extra-virgin olive oil

2 tablespoons chopped garlic

2 tablespoons freshly squeezed lemon juice

1½ tablespoons fresh rosemary leaves

2 teaspoons freshly ground black pepper

1 teaspoon paprika

1 teaspoon Worcestershire sauce

1 teaspoon kosher salt

Neutral cooking oil, for oiling the grill grates

24 extra-jumbo (U16/20) shrimp, tail-on, peeled, and deveined

TIP

This sauce is also delicious brushed on other grilled shell-fish, such as lobster or scallops.

1. In a saucepan over medium heat, melt the butter and olive oil together. Add the garlic and lightly sauté for 1 to 2 minutes, until tender. Stir in the lemon juice, rosemary, pepper, paprika, Worcestershire sauce, and salt. Simmer for 2 to 3 minutes.

2. Prepare the grill for direct grilling and bring the temperature to medium-high heat (400°F to 450°F). Brush the cooking grates clean.

3. Oil the cooking grates, then place the shrimp over direct heat. Cook, uncovered, for 1 to 3 minutes per side, until the shrimp turn bright pink.

4. Immediately place the cooked shrimp in the warm sauce and toss thoroughly until well coated. Serve immediately.

Garlic and Lime Shrimp

SERVES 4

PREP TIME:
15 minutes,
plus
30 minutes
to marinate

COOK TIME:
5 minutest

*This versatile shrimp dish bursts with flavor from a hint
of heat and tartness. These shrimp are also delicious
served with toasted bread rubbed with garlic cloves.*

1 small jalapeño pepper,
  stemmed
¼ cup freshly squeezed lime
  juice
4 garlic cloves, finely chopped
1 tablespoon chili powder
1 teaspoon olive oil

1 teaspoon salt
24 extra-jumbo (U16/20)
  shrimp, tail-on, peeled, and
  deveined
Neutral cooking oil, for oiling
  the grill grates

1. In a blender, combine the jalapeño, lime juice, garlic, chili
   powder, olive oil, and salt. Puree until smooth. Put the shrimp in
   a large shallow bowl and pour the marinade over them. Cover
   and let sit at room temperature for 30 minutes.

2. Prepare the grill for direct grilling and bring the temperature
   to medium-high heat (400°F to 450°F). Brush the cooking
   grates clean.

3. Oil the cooking grates, then place the shrimp over direct heat.
   Cook, uncovered, for 1 to 3 minutes per side, until the shrimp
   turn bright pink. Serve immediately.

TIP

*Garnish the shrimp
with lime or lemon
slices, cherry tomatoes,
and a few sprigs
of basil.*

Oysters with Lemon-Garlic Sauce

SERVES 4

PREP TIME:
15 minutes

COOK TIME:
15 minutes

Grilled oysters are every bit as delicious as raw ones. This version delivers with a buttery lemon-garlic sauce to complement the subtle briny flavor oysters are known for.

8 tablespoons (1 stick)
  unsalted butter
4 garlic cloves, minced
2 tablespoons freshly
  squeezed lemon juice
¼ teaspoon salt

¼ teaspoon black pepper
Neutral cooking oil, for oiling
  the grill grates
24 fresh oysters, rinsed and
  cleaned

TIP

~~~~~

Substitute medium-neck clams for the oysters and cook for the same amount of time.

1. Melt the butter in a saucepan over medium heat. Add the garlic and cook for 1 to 2 minutes, until tender. Stir in the lemon juice, salt, and pepper. Simmer the sauce for 3 to 4 minutes, then set aside until ready to serve.

2. Prepare the grill for direct grilling and bring the temperature to medium-high heat (400°F to 450°F). Brush the cooking grates clean.

3. Oil the cooking grates, then place the oysters over direct heat and close the lid. Cook for 4 to 6 minutes, turning every 2 to 3 minutes, until the oyster shells pop open. Then cook for about 2 minutes more and remove from the grill. Discard any oysters that have not opened. Serve the oysters with the lemon-garlic sauce on the side for dipping.

Barbecue-Rubbed Salmon Fillets

SERVES 4

PREP TIME:
15 minutes

COOK TIME:
5 minutes

Salmon is delicate in texture but hearty in taste due to its oiliness. Adding a simple barbecue rub provides just the right contrast to the smooth, rich taste of the salmon.

¼ cup paprika

2 tablespoons packed light brown sugar

1 tablespoon salt

1 tablespoon freshly ground black pepper

1 tablespoon chili powder

1 tablespoon garlic powder

1 tablespoon onion powder

4 (6-ounce) salmon fillets, skinned

2 tablespoons extra-virgin olive oil

Neutral cooking oil, for oiling the grill grates

TIP

Store the leftover rub in an airtight container in a cool, dark place for up to 6 months.

1. In a small bowl, stir together the paprika, brown sugar, salt, pepper, chili powder, garlic powder, and onion powder until blended. Brush each salmon fillet with olive oil and sprinkle a generous amount of barbecue rub on each side of the salmon fillets.

2. Prepare the grill for direct grilling and bring the temperature to medium-high heat (400°F to 450°F). Brush the cooking grates clean.

3. Oil the cooking grates, then place the salmon fillets over direct heat. Cook, uncovered, for 2 to 3 minutes per side, until the salmon turns bright pink. Remove from the heat and serve.

Tandoori-Spiced Sea Bass

SERVES 4

PREP TIME:
15 minutes,
plus
20 minutes
to marinate

COOK TIME:
10 minutes

Sea bass is a mild, firm-textured fish that works exceptionally well with spicy rubs and sauces. This recipe is a twist on traditional tandoori-style sea bass with a much shorter prep time.

1 tablespoon paprika
2 teaspoons ground cumin
1 teaspoon ground coriander
1 teaspoon ground turmeric
1 teaspoon garam masala
½ teaspoon cayenne pepper
½ teaspoon black pepper

½ teaspoon salt
1 tablespoon olive oil
4 (6- to 8-ounce) sea bass
  fillets, skinned
Neutral cooking oil, for oiling
  the grill grates

1. In a small bowl, stir together the paprika, cumin, coriander, turmeric, garam masala, cayenne pepper, black pepper, and salt until blended. Brush the olive oil on all sides of the sea bass fillets. Sprinkle a generous amount of rub on the fillets until well coated on both sides. Cover with plastic wrap and refrigerate for 20 minutes.

2. Prepare the grill for direct grilling and bring the temperature to medium-high heat (400°F to 450°F). Brush the cooking grates clean.

3. Oil the cooking grates, then place the sea bass over direct heat. Cook, uncovered, for 3 to 4 minutes per side, until the fish is firm to the touch.

4. Remove from the heat and serve immediately.

TIP

Instead of the cumin, coriander, turmeric, and garam masala, use 3 tablespoons of curry powder plus the paprika and cayenne pepper as indicated and mix before sprinkling on the sea bass.

Halibut with Tomatoes and Herbs

SERVES 4

PREP TIME:
15 minutes

COOK TIME:
10 minutes

Virgin sauce, or sauce vierge, is a traditional French topping for seafood and chicken. The brightness of the tomatoes and herbs complements the firm, flaky texture of the halibut.

½ cup extra-virgin olive oil

4 Roma tomatoes, diced

¼ cup chopped fresh basil leaves

¼ cup chopped fresh parsley

2 tablespoons freshly squeezed lemon juice

½ teaspoon salt, plus more for seasoning

¼ teaspoon black pepper, plus more for seasoning

4 (6- to 8-ounce) halibut fillets

Neutral cooking oil, for oiling the grill grates

1. In a medium bowl, mix the olive oil, tomatoes, basil, parsley, lemon juice, salt, and pepper to combine. Cover and set aside at room temperature until ready to serve.

2. Season each halibut fillet with a pinch of salt and pepper.

3. Prepare the grill for direct grilling and bring the temperature to medium-high heat (400°F to 450°F). Brush the cooking grates clean.

4. Oil the cooking grates, then place the halibut fillets over direct heat. Cook, uncovered, for 3 to 4 minutes per side, until the fish is tender and white.

5. Top each halibut fillet with the tomato-herb sauce and serve.

TIP

This sauce can also be used with other firm fish, such as grouper or monkfish.

Red Snapper with Creamy Lemon Sauce

SERVES 4

PREP TIME:
15 minutes

COOK TIME:
15 minutes

Red snapper is a perfect match for this tangy and creamy lemon sauce. Pair this bright dish with a crisp salad and a warm baguette.

½ cup dry white wine
Juice of 1 lemon
1 shallot, minced
8 tablespoons (1 stick) unsalted butter, cut into 6 equal pieces
½ cup heavy (whipping) cream

4 (6- to 8-ounce) red snapper fillets
Olive oil, for brushing
Pinch salt
Pinch black pepper
Neutral cooking oil, for oiling the grill grates

TIP

Red snapper may be difficult to find at some grocery chains. Substitute tilapia if needed.

1. In a small saucepan over medium heat, combine the wine, lemon juice, and shallot. Cook for 1 to 2 minutes. Turn the heat to low and add the butter, one piece at a time, stirring constantly, until smooth and creamy. Remove from the heat and slowly whisk in the heavy cream until blended. Return the saucepan to low heat and cook for about 5 minutes, until thickened. Remove from the heat and set aside.

2. Brush all sides of each snapper fillet with olive oil, then sprinkle with salt and pepper.

3. Prepare the grill for direct grilling and bring the temperature to medium-high heat (400°F to 450°F). Brush the cooking grates clean.

4. Oil the cooking grates, then place the red snapper fillets over direct heat. Cook, uncovered, for 2 to 3 minutes per side, until the fish is firm. Remove from the heat and serve the snapper bathed in the lemon sauce.

Rainbow Trout with Almond Butter Sauce

SERVES 4

PREP TIME:
15 minutes

COOK TIME:
15 minutes

Rainbow trout is a soft, delicate fish that benefits from seasonings that don't overwhelm its sweet flavor. You'll find a similar version of this recipe at higher-end restaurants, but it won't taste as good as the one you make yourself.

½ cup slivered almonds
4 tablespoons (½ stick)
  unsalted butter
1 teaspoon salt
1 teaspoon freshly ground
  black pepper

¼ cup dry white wine
Neutral cooking oil, for oiling
  the grill grates
4 (4- to 6-ounce) rainbow
  trout fillets

TIP

Add a flourish of chopped parsley right before serving for some added freshness.

1. Heat a medium nonstick or cast-iron skillet over medium heat for 3 to 4 minutes. Pour in the almonds and toast for 4 to 5 minutes, gently stirring every minute, until they turn golden brown.

2. In a small saucepan over low heat, combine the butter, salt, and pepper. Heat until the butter melts, then turn the heat to high and add the white wine. Cook, stirring constantly, until the sauce comes to a rolling boil. Remove from the heat and set aside.

3. Prepare the grill for direct grilling and bring the temperature to medium heat (350°F to 400°F). Brush the cooking grates clean.

4. Oil the cooking grates, then place the trout fillets, skin-side down, over direct heat and close the lid. Cook for 5 to 6 minutes—do not turn the fish. Transfer the trout fillets to a serving plate. Spoon the sauce over the fish and sprinkle with the toasted almonds to serve.

Mahi-Mahi with Sweet-and-Sour Glaze

SERVES 4

PREP TIME:
15 minutes

COOK TIME:
15 minutes

Mahi-mahi is a flaky and flavorful fish that is made for the grill. This sweet-and-sour glaze creates the perfect finish. Serve with grilled veggies for a delicious and nutritious meal.

⅓ cup sugar
3 tablespoons rice vinegar
2 tablespoons freshly squeezed lime juice
1 tablespoon soy sauce
1 teaspoon peeled and grated fresh ginger
⅓ cup dry white wine

2 teaspoons cornstarch
4 (6- to 8-ounce) mahi-mahi fillets
1 teaspoon salt
1 teaspoon freshly ground black pepper
Neutral cooking oil, for oiling the grill grates

TIP

Make the glaze the day before to make this dish come together even faster.

1. In a small saucepan over low heat, combine the sugar, vinegar, lime juice, soy sauce, and ginger. Cook until the sugar melts, about 2 minutes, then turn the heat to medium.

2. In a small bowl, whisk together the wine and cornstarch, add it to the sauce, and bring to a boil. Cook for 2 minutes more, until the glaze thickens. Remove from the heat and set aside.

3. Lightly season each fillet with the salt and pepper, then brush with the glaze.

4. Prepare the grill for direct grilling and bring the temperature to medium heat (350°F to 400°F). Brush the cooking grates clean.

5. Oil the cooking grates, then place the mahi-mahi over direct heat and close the lid. Cook for 4 to 5 minutes per side, until the fish is light in color and the juices run off the fillet, brushing the glaze on the fish once per turn. Remove from the heat and serve with additional glaze on the side.

Sesame-Crusted Tuna with Wasabi Sauce

SERVES 4

This classic is perfect for sushi lovers and is ready quick.

PREP TIME:
15 minutes

COOK TIME:
10 minutes

4 tablespoons (½ stick)
   unsalted butter
¼ cup dry white wine
1 tablespoon minced shallot
3 tablespoons soy sauce
2 tablespoons wasabi paste

½ cup sesame seeds
4 (6- to 8-ounce) ahi tuna
   steaks
1 tablespoon olive oil
Neutral cooking oil, for oiling
   the grill grates

1. In a small saucepan over medium heat, melt the butter. Add the wine and shallot. Cook for 1 to 2 minutes, then bring to a simmer and cook for 3 to 4 minutes more. Whisk in the soy sauce and wasabi paste and remove from the heat.

2. Pour the sesame seeds onto a small plate. Brush the tuna steaks with the olive oil and place each tuna steak in the seeds, turning to cover the entire surface.

3. Prepare the grill for direct grilling and bring the temperature to medium-high heat (400°F to 450°F). Brush the cooking grates clean.

4. Oil the cooking grates, then place the tuna over direct heat. Cook, uncovered, for 2 minutes per side, until the sesame seeds turn golden brown. Do not overcook the tuna, or it will become tough.

5. Place the tuna steaks on a large cutting board. Cut into ¼-inch-thick slices and transfer to a serving plate. Serve the wasabi sauce on the side.

TIP

Add more heat to this dish if you want it spicy: Sprinkle chopped jalapeño pepper and fresh cilantro over the sliced tuna just before serving.

Bacon-Basil Scallops

SERVES 4

PREP TIME:
20 minutes

COOK TIME:
15 minutes

Scallops and bacon are a popular combination—and for good reason. The sweet and delicate flavor of the scallops pairs well with the saltiness of the bacon. Fresh sweet basil provides the perfect counterbalance to the bacon.

4 bacon slices
2 pounds medium sea
   scallops
¼ cup extra-virgin olive oil
2 tablespoons freshly
   squeezed lemon juice

1 teaspoon freshly ground
   black pepper
Neutral cooking oil, for oiling
   the grill grates
½ cup fresh basil leaves, cut
   into thin ribbons

TIP

This recipe can be adapted to shrimp; plan on 6 large shrimp per person.

1. In a large skillet over medium heat, cook the bacon for 8 to 10 minutes, until crisp. Transfer it with tongs to a paper towel–lined plate to drain and cool. Chop the bacon and set it aside.

2. Rinse the scallops and place them on a paper towel–lined plate to drain. Dry well with paper towels.

3. In a small bowl, whisk together the olive oil, lemon juice, and pepper to blend. Set it aside for serving.

4. Prepare the grill for direct grilling and bring the temperature to medium-high heat (400°F to 450°F). Brush the cooking grates clean.

5. Oil the cooking grates, then place the scallops over direct heat. Cook, uncovered, for 2 to 3 minutes per side, just until the scallops are firm—no longer. Transfer the scallops to a serving plate and sprinkle with the cooked bacon and the basil. Spoon the sauce over the scallops and serve immediately.

Miso-Glazed Cod and Bok Choy

SERVES 4

PREP TIME:
10 minutes

COOK TIME:
15 minutes

A tangy, sweet, umami-rich glaze is brushed on tender fillets of cod and leafy bok choy, which are all grilled until tender, creating a delightfully, slightly sticky exterior.

¼ cup miso paste

¼ cup sake

3 tablespoons packed light brown sugar

2 tablespoons rice wine vinegar

1½ tablespoons soy sauce

½ teaspoon sriracha

Kosher salt

Freshly ground black pepper

4 (6-ounce) cod fillets, skin-on

4 baby bok choy, halved lengthwise and thoroughly washed

Neutral cooking oil, for oiling the grill grates

1. Prepare the grill and bring the temperature to medium-high heat (400°F to 450°F).

2. In a small bowl, whisk together the miso, sake, sugar, vinegar, soy sauce, sriracha, and a pinch of salt and pepper.

3. Season the cod fillets and bok choy with salt and pepper and generously brush the fillets and bok choy with the glaze.

4. Oil the cooking grates, then grill the cod, skin-side down, for 4 minutes. Brush on more glaze after 2 minutes. Flip and grill for 2 to 4 minutes, until the cod's internal temperature reaches 130°F and it flakes when poked gently.

5. Grill the bok choy over direct heat, cut-side down, until lightly charred, about 45 seconds. Flip, transfer to indirect heat, brush on more glaze, and grill until tender when poked with a knife, 2 to 3 minutes more.

TIP

Halibut, mahi-mahi, striped bass, or red snapper would make a delicious substitute for cod.

Crispy Sardines with Pimenta Moida

**SERVES
4 TO 6**

PREP TIME:
2 minutes

COOK TIME:
20 minutes

Simple to prepare, these delicious little fish need no prep beyond washing and a bit of seasoning. Serve them with some crusty bread and a cold glass of crisp white wine.

12 fresh or thawed sardines, rinsed

1 teaspoon avocado oil

1 teaspoon Pimenta Moida (page 218)

½ teaspoon sea salt

Nonstick cooking spray

1. In a large bowl, mix the sardines, avocado oil, Pimenta Moida, and salt with your hands, working the seasoning into the fish.
2. Set a gas grill to medium or set up a charcoal grill for indirect heat. Spray the grill rack with nonstick cooking spray. Grill the sardines until the skin starts to break, about 10 minutes per side.
3. Transfer to a serving platter and serve.

TIP

For easier grilling, consider purchasing an inexpensive grill basket with a handle for flipping.

Swordfish with Chimichurri and Roasted Vegetables

SERVES 4

PREP TIME:
10 minutes

COOK TIME:
20 minutes

Swordfish pairs beautifully with bright, herbaceous chimichurri. This chimichurri is delightful spooned over most any fish, meat, or vegetables.

½ cup tightly packed chopped fresh parsley

¼ cup coarsely chopped fresh oregano

1 cup diced red onion, divided

4 garlic cloves, peeled

¼ cup red wine vinegar

½ cup extra-virgin olive oil, plus 1½ tablespoons, plus more for brushing

1 tablespoon red pepper flakes

Kosher salt

Freshly ground black pepper

1 zucchini, halved lengthwise and sliced

1 small head cauliflower, cut into florets

1 large carrot, sliced

4 (6-ounce) swordfish steaks

1. For the chimichurri sauce, place the parsley, oregano, ½ cup of onion, the garlic, vinegar, ½ cup of olive oil, the red pepper flakes, and a pinch of salt and black pepper in a food processor. Pulse several times until combined, leaving some chunks in the mixture. Transfer to a ramekin or serving bowl to allow the flavors to combine.

2. Preheat the oven to 400°F.

3. In a large bowl, toss the zucchini, cauliflower, carrot, the remaining ½ cup of onion, and the remaining 1½ tablespoons of olive oil. Season with salt and black pepper. Arrange in a single layer on a large baking sheet and roast for 15 to 20 minutes, to your preferred doneness.

Continued on next page ⟶

4. Meanwhile, heat the grill or a stove-top grill pan to medium-high heat. Brush the swordfish steaks with olive oil and season with salt and pepper. Grill for 5 to 6 minutes on each side, depending on thickness.

5. Put one swordfish steak on each plate with a quarter of the vegetables. Top with the chimichurri sauce and serve immediately.

TIP

Prepare additional chimichurri sauce to serve on top of the vegetables or use for dipping.

Grilled Lobster with Citrusy Garlic Butter

SERVES 4

PREP TIME:
15 minutes

COOK TIME:
15 minutes

In this recipe, succulent lobster is grilled and generously brushed with citrusy butter with notes of lemon, orange, garlic, serrano chile, and lots of herbs. Throw some crusty bread on the grill and whip up a simple side salad for a fancy dinner.

8 tablespoons (1 stick) unsalted butter, melted

2 red serrano chiles, seeded, pith removed, and minced

4 garlic cloves, minced

2 tablespoons minced chives

2 tablespoons chopped fresh parsley

1 tablespoon lemon zest

1 tablespoon freshly squeezed lemon juice

1 tablespoon orange zest

1 tablespoon freshly squeezed orange juice

Kosher salt

Freshly ground black pepper

4 (8-ounce) lobster tails

Olive oil, for brushing

1. Prepare a grill and bring the temperature to medium heat (350°F to 400°F). If using wooden skewers, soak them in water for 30 minutes.

2. In a small bowl, whisk together the melted butter, chiles, garlic, chives, parsley, lemon zest, lemon juice, orange zest, orange juice, and a pinch of salt and pepper. Transfer half of the butter to a separate bowl and set aside for brushing the tails.

3. Using kitchen shears, cut the top of the lobster shell from the meaty part of the tail. With a paring knife, cut lengthwise down the center, a little less than halfway through the meat, being careful not to cut all the way through. Insert a skewer through the meat lengthwise. This will prevent the meat from curling when cooking.

4. Brush the tails with oil and season with salt and pepper. Grill meat-side down until lightly charred, 5 to 6 minutes. Flip and generously brush with the reserved butter. Grill until just barely cooked through, 4 to 5 minutes more.

5. Serve with the remaining citrusy garlic butter.

TIP

This butter is a multi-purpose workhorse. Slather it on shrimp, scallops, or any seafood fillet.

8

STAPLES

Creole Salsa

**MAKES
4 CUPS**

PREP TIME:
20 minutes

This chunky salsa offers mild heat with the addition of green chiles.

1 bunch cilantro leaves, coarsely chopped
8 garlic cloves, peeled
4 Roma tomatoes, cut into large chunks
1 medium red onion, cut into large chunks
2 jalapeño peppers, sliced
1 (4.5-ounce) can diced green chiles
½ cup chopped scallions, white and green parts

Juice of 1 lime
1 tablespoon olive oil
½ tablespoon Cajun Spice Blend (page 217)
½ tablespoon Worcestershire sauce
1 teaspoon garlic salt
1 cup crushed tomatoes
1 cup tomato-based chili sauce
Tortilla chips or vegetable chips, for serving

1. Place the cilantro and garlic in a food processor and pulse until finely chopped.

2. Add the tomatoes, red onion, jalapeño peppers, chiles, scallions, lime juice, olive oil, Cajun spice blend, Worcestershire sauce, and garlic salt. Pulse several times, until the tomatoes and onion are coarsely chopped and all the ingredients are well mixed.

3. Transfer the mixture to a large bowl, then add the crushed tomatoes and chili sauce. Stir well to incorporate.

4. Transfer the salsa to a bowl and serve with tortilla chips or vegetable chips.

TIP

Store in an airtight container in the refrigerator for up to 5 days. It will be delicious chilled, but it's also great heated up and served warm as a sauce, particularly over rice, poached eggs, or grilled tuna or swordfish.

Cajun Spice Blend

MAKES
¼ CUP

PREP TIME:
10 minutes

This blend of cayenne pepper, black pepper, and white pepper combined with garlic powder, onion powder, and dry mustard provides the distinctive heat and flavor found in many Cajun dishes.

2 tablespoons kosher salt

½ tablespoon cayenne pepper

½ tablespoon freshly ground
   black pepper

½ tablespoon white pepper

½ tablespoon garlic powder

½ tablespoon onion powder

½ tablespoon dry mustard

In a medium bowl, combine the salt, cayenne pepper, black pepper, white pepper, garlic powder, onion powder, and dry mustard and stir until mixed.

TIP

For a finer consistency, put all the ingredients in a food processor and pulse for a few seconds. Store in an airtight container or a Mason jar with a screw-top lid. This blend will keep for several months in the pantry. Feel free to double or triple the recipe if you plan on using more than ¼ cup within 2 months.

Pimenta Moida

MAKES 2 TO 3 CUPS

PREP TIME: 1 hour

COOK TIME: 48 to 96 hours to ferment, plus 72 hours to rest

No sauce is more classic Portuguese than Pimenta Moida. It's a sauce made of chile peppers that are ground and then left to ferment. Try it as a piquant topping for sandwiches, stews, and vegetables.

24 hot red peppers
½ cup kosher salt, plus more for topping

2 tablespoons preserving powder, like ascorbic acid

1. While wearing latex or rubber gloves, wash and dry the peppers. Cut the peppers in half lengthwise and remove the stems and seeds.

2. Using an old-fashioned grinder or the grinder attachment on a stand mixer, grind the peppers into a large stainless-steel bowl. Add the salt, stir to combine, and cover the bowl with a clean dishcloth.

TIP

~~~~~~

This sauce is relatively mild, but if you prefer something a little spicier, leave a few seeds in the mix.

3. Let the bowl sit at room temperature for 24 to 72 hours. The peppers will ferment or boil, a process that uses the heat from the capsaicin in the pepper itself. When you observe a reduction in the boiling, add the preserving powder and stir to combine.

4. Let the mixture sit at room temperature, covered, for an additional 24 hours. Stir again and transfer the mixture to sanitized containers like canning jars. Place the lids on loosely. Let sit for an additional 72 hours.

5. Tighten the lids and store the containers at room temperature. Once a jar is opened, store it in the refrigerator for up to 8 months.

Portuguese Allspice

**MAKES
ABOUT
½ CUP**

PREP TIME:
10 minutes

COOK TIME:
25 minutes

Portuguese allspice may be hard to find in some markets, but it can be made at home. Note that this is nothing like the whole spice, which is not a blend.

Grated zest of 1 orange
¼ cup sweet paprika
1 tablespoon granulated garlic

1 teaspoon ground turmeric
1 teaspoon onion powder
½ teaspoon freshly ground white pepper

1. Preheat the oven to 275°F. Line a baking sheet with parchment paper.
2. Place the zest on the prepared sheet and bake for 25 minutes, or until the zest is dried. Let the zest cool completely, then, using a spice grinder, grind it into a powder.
3. In a small Mason jar or an airtight container, mix the ground zest, paprika, granulated garlic, turmeric, onion powder, and white pepper. Cover with a lid and shake to mix thoroughly.
4. Store the spice mixture in a sealed jar for up to 1 week at room temperature.

TIP

Add ½ teaspoon of spice mixture to onion and garlic sautéed in olive oil and you are well on your way to infusing Portuguese flavors into almost any protein. Just be careful not to overdo it; you don't want to overpower the dish's flavor.

Gravlax

**SERVES
6 TO 8**

PREP TIME:
15 minutes,
plus 3 days to
cure

Curing fish was one of the many methods used to preserve it before the invention of the refrigerator. Gravlax is the easiest and quickest method, using a simple mix of salt, sugar, and a few spices for extra flavor and allowing time and osmosis to do the work. If you can't find juniper berries, use yellow mustard seeds instead.

1 (8-ounce) salmon fillet, skin-on and pin bones removed

1 teaspoon whole black peppercorns

1 teaspoon whole juniper berries

2 tablespoons freshly squeezed lemon juice

1½ tablespoons kosher salt

1½ tablespoons sugar

1 tablespoon coarsely chopped fresh dill

1 tablespoon gin or vodka

1. Rinse the salmon under cold water and blot dry with paper towels. Place the salmon, skin-side down, in a baking dish.

2. With a mortar and pestle, coarsely crack the peppercorns and juniper berries a few times. Transfer them to a small bowl and mix with the lemon juice, salt, sugar, dill, and gin.

3. Spread the spice mixture over the top of the salmon and cover with plastic wrap. Refrigerate for 3 days undisturbed.

4. Remove the gravlax from the baking dish and rinse off the curing mixture. Blot the fish dry with paper towels.

5. Using a sharp knife, slice the gravlax into paper-thin slices and serve cold. The gravlax can be stored in the refrigerator tightly wrapped in plastic for up to 5 days.

TIP

Add 1 teaspoon of minced fresh jalapeño and 1 tablespoon of cilantro instead of the dill for a spicy twist.

Briny, Punchy Tartar Sauce

**MAKES
2 CUPS**

PREP TIME:
5 minutes

A dip for fish and chips might be the most obvious choice for this bright tartar sauce, but it is also delicious alongside crab cakes and salmon cakes and makes a great sauce for crispy fish or shrimp sandwiches.

1½ cups mayonnaise
¾ cup finely chopped dill pickles
3 tablespoons capers, roughly chopped
2 tablespoons minced onion
2 tablespoons roughly chopped fresh dill

1½ teaspoons lemon zest
1 tablespoon freshly squeezed lemon juice
1 large garlic clove, minced
Kosher salt
Freshly ground black pepper

1. In a medium bowl, mix the mayonnaise, pickles, capers, onion, dill, lemon zest, lemon juice, and garlic. Season with salt and pepper to taste.
2. Refrigerate in a sealed container for up to 1 week.

TIP

A dash of sriracha makes a deliciously spicy version.

Chimichurri

MAKES
1½ CUPS

PREP TIME:
10 minutes

One of the more flavorful and versatile sauces, Chimichurri is perfect in its simplicity. This vinaigrette-adjacent sauce of fresh parsley, spicy chiles, garlic, red wine vinegar, oil, salt, and pepper instantly elevates fish, shellfish, grilled vegetables, even chicken or steak.

¾ cup finely chopped fresh parsley

4 garlic cloves, minced

2 red serrano chiles or Anaheim chiles, seeded and pith removed

2 tablespoons red wine vinegar

1½ teaspoons lemon zest

1 tablespoon freshly squeezed lemon juice

½ cup extra-virgin olive oil

Kosher salt

Freshly ground black pepper

In a small bowl, mix the parsley, garlic, chiles, red wine vinegar, lemon zest, and lemon juice. Slowly stream in the olive oil while whisking constantly. Season with salt and pepper.

TIP

Chimichurri can be
made 1 day in
advance and stored
in an airtight jar in
the refrigerator for
up to 1 week.

Citrus-Caper Salsa

**MAKES
2½ CUPS**

PREP TIME:
20 minutes

*The bright, punchy flavors in this citrus salsa, studded
with capers, are perfect for highlighting almost any fish.
This version features a trio of citrus fruits, but feel free to
substitute with what you have on hand.*

1 orange
1 grapefruit
1 lemon
¼ cup roughly chopped fresh
   parsley
1 tablespoon capers, roughly
   chopped

1 small shallot, minced
1 garlic clove, minced
2 tablespoons extra-virgin
   olive oil
Kosher salt
Freshly ground black pepper

1. Cut the ends off of the orange,
   grapefruit, and lemon. Place
   each fruit flat-side down on
   a cutting board. Remove the
   rind from the fruit. If some pith
   remains, use a paring knife to
   remove it. Observe where the
   fruit is separated by membranes
   into segments. Set each fruit on
   its side. Cut along a membrane toward the center, repeating
   the same technique with the adjacent membrane until the cuts
   meet, releasing the citrus segment. Repeat with the remaining
   fruit until it is all divided into segments.

2. Place the citrus segments in a medium bowl, along with the
   parsley, capers, shallot, garlic, and olive oil. Season with salt and
   pepper. Gently toss to combine. Cover and refrigerate for up
   to 3 days.

TIP

*After supreming citrus,
the fruit will still have a ton
of leftover juice. Squeeze
the pieces and save the
juice for a marinade,
vinaigrette,
or sauce.*

Citrusy Compound Butter

**MAKES
1 LOG**

PREP TIME:
10 minutes

Compound butter is a wonderful way to give proteins and vegetables a flavorful punch. Even better, it can be made in advance and tailored to fit the flavor profile of any dish (see tip). This citrusy version with garlic and herbs is delicious for finishing grilled or roasted fish and vegetables.

8 tablespoons (1 stick) unsalted butter, at room temperature

2 tablespoons freshly squeezed lemon juice

2 tablespoons chopped fresh thyme

1 tablespoon chopped fresh rosemary

2 teaspoons orange zest

2 teaspoons lemon zest

2 garlic cloves, minced

Kosher salt

Freshly ground black pepper

1. In a food processor, place the butter, lemon juice, thyme, rosemary, orange zest, lemon zest, and garlic and lightly pulse to combine. Season with salt and pepper.

2. Spoon the butter onto a sheet of plastic wrap or parchment paper. Using the sides to help you, gather the butter to the center and roll it into a log, twisting the ends of the plastic to seal it.

3. Wrap in a layer of parchment paper and refrigerate for up to 1 month.

TIP

Here are a few other combo ideas to get you started (add these to the food processor in step 1): 2 finely chopped chiles; sea salt with rosemary, thyme, oregano, and basil; feta and herb butter (omit the orange zest and add ¼ cup of crumbled feta); miso and lemon; or sun-dried tomatoes and balsamic vinegar. The options are truly endless.

Lemon-Garlic Aioli

**MAKES
2 CUPS**

PREP TIME:
5 minutes

A condiment you can slather on almost anything, this garlic aioli is especially delightful on fried fish, potatoes, and veggies. Try a swipe alongside grilled or roasted fish and vegetables for a spicy, citrusy, creamy kick.

2 cups mayonnaise
2 tablespoons freshly
  squeezed lemon juice
2 teaspoons lemon zest

2 large garlic cloves, minced
Kosher salt
Freshly ground black pepper

In a medium bowl, mix the mayonnaise, lemon juice, lemon zest, and garlic. Season with salt and pepper to taste.

TIP

Make this 1 day in advance and store it in an airtight jar for up to 2 weeks.

Measurement Conversions

VOLUME EQUIVALENTS	U.S. STANDARD	U.S. STANDARD (OUNCES)	METRIC (APPROXIMATE)
LIQUID	2 tablespoons	1 fl. oz.	30 mL
	¼ cup	2 fl. oz.	60 mL
	½ cup	4 fl. oz.	120 mL
	1 cup	8 fl. oz.	240 mL
	1½ cups	12 fl. oz.	355 mL
	2 cups or 1 pint	16 fl. oz.	475 mL
	4 cups or 1 quart	32 fl. oz.	1 L
	1 gallon	128 fl. oz.	4 L
DRY	⅛ teaspoon	–	0.5 mL
	¼ teaspoon	–	1 mL
	½ teaspoon	–	2 mL
	¾ teaspoon	–	4 mL
	1 teaspoon	–	5 mL
	1 tablespoon	–	15 mL
	¼ cup	–	59 mL
	⅓ cup	–	79 mL
	½ cup	–	118 mL
	⅔ cup	–	156 mL
	¾ cup	–	177 mL
	1 cup	–	235 mL
	2 cups or 1 pint	–	475 mL
	3 cups	–	700 mL
	4 cups or 1 quart	–	1 L
	½ gallon	–	2 L
	1 gallon	–	4 L

OVEN TEMPERATURES

FAHRENHEIT	CELSIUS (APPROXIMATE)
250°F	120°C
300°F	150°C
325°F	165°C
350°F	180°C
375°F	190°C
400°F	200°C
425°F	220°C
450°F	230°C

WEIGHT EQUIVALENTS

U.S. STANDARD	METRIC (APPROXIMATE)
½ ounce	15 g
1 ounce	30 g
2 ounces	60 g
4 ounces	115 g
8 ounces	225 g
12 ounces	340 g
16 ounces or 1 pound	455 g

Sustainability Resources

Aquaculture Stewardship Council: ASC-Aqua.org

Environmental Working Group's (EWG) Consumer Guide to Seafood provides user-friendly background data on which fish are best to consume, both health-wise and environmentally: EWG.org/consumer-guides/ewgs-consumer-guide-seafood

FoodPrint: FoodPrint.org

Grocery Store Sustainability Guides: Most grocers have resources on sustainable seafood, which you can find on your grocery store's website. I often consult my local store's sustainability guide: HEB.com/static-page/Sustainable-Seafood-at-HEB

Marine Stewardship Council: MSC.org/en-us

Monterey Bay Aquarium's Seafood Watch is an extremely comprehensive resource with detailed information about where our seafood comes from and how it is sourced, broken down by location and methodology. Their charts lay out which types of seafood are best, which ones are certified and good alternatives, and which ones should be avoided: SeafoodWatch.org

World Wildlife Fund's Seafood Sustainability Resources: SeafoodSustainability.org/resources

Index

Acknowledgments

This unique project would not have been possible without the team at Callisto Media and the many amazing collaborators, primarily the authors of *The Big 10 Fish and Seafood Cookbook*, *The Easy Puerto Rican Cookbook*, *Essential Seafood Cookbook*, *The Easy Creole and Cajun Cookbook*, *The Easy 5-Ingredient Pescatarian Cookbook*, *French Cooking for Beginners*, *The Best of New Orleans Cookbook*, *The 28-Day Pescatarian Meal Plan & Cookbook*, *The 30-Minute Mediterranean Diet Cookbook*, *Easy Portuguese Cookbook*, *The Pescatarian Cookbook for Beginners*, *One-Pot Mediterranean Diet*, and *How to Grill for Beginners*. Thank you for helping such a comprehensive seafood cookbook come together.

About the Author

 **DANI COLOMBATTO** is a recipe developer, the voice of the blog *Dani Goes South*, and the author of *The 30-Minute Pescatarian Cookbook*, released in 2020. Dani resides in Austin, Texas, with her fiancé, Benjamin, and cats, Greg and Lou. If she's not in the kitchen or shooting recipes, you can most likely find her gardening or in the thick of a home-sprucing project with Ben. She thanks you warmly for giving this book a read and greatly hopes you find a recipe you love inside.

CPSIA information can be obtained
at www.ICGtesting.com
Printed in the USA
JSHW041640250222
23356JS00003B/3